Mystical Words

The Magick of The Heart, The Soul, and The Empowered Mind

DAMON BRAND

Copyright © 2019 Damon Brand

All Rights Reserved. This book may not be reproduced, in whole or in part, in any form or by any means electronic or mechanical, including photocopying, recording, or by any information storage retrieval system now known or hereafter invented, without written permission from the publisher, The Gallery of Magick.

It is hereby expressly stated that the images in this book may not be reproduced in any form, except for individual and personal use. Derivative works based on these images or the associated concepts are not permitted, and any such attempt to create a derivative work will be met with legal action.

Disclaimer: Consider all information in this book to be speculation and not professional advice, to be used at your own risk. Damon Brand and The Gallery of Magick are not responsible for the consequences of your actions should you choose to use the methods in this book. Success depends on the integrity of your workings, the initial conditions of your life, and your natural abilities so results will vary. The information is never intended to replace or substitute for medical advice from a professional practitioner, and when it comes to issues of physical health, mental health or emotional conditions, no advice is given or implied, and you should always seek conventional, professional advice. The information is provided on the understanding that you will use it in accordance with the laws of your country.

CONTENTS

Introduction: The Mystical Adventure	9
Part One: The Mystical Words	11
The Method	15
The Pleasure	17
The Changes	21
How this Magick Works	23
The Attuning Ritual	27
The Practice of Magick	31
Receiving the Magick	37
The Ritual of Perception	41
The Ritual of Knowledge	45
The Ritual of Imagination	49
The Ritual of Love	53
The Ritual of Healing	57
The Ritual of Transformation	61
The Ritual of The Empowered Mind	65
Experiencing the Mystical	69
Part Two: World Changing	71
Be Seen by Those You Care About	76
Be Seen in a Chosen Way	78
Become More Noticeable to People	80
Experience Improved Intuition	82
Find Clarity When Confused	84
Influence with Emotions	86
Appear Trustworthy	88
Attract Through Inner Light	90
Attract a Following	92
Find Hope in a Difficult Time	94
Catch a Glimpse of Possible Futures	96
Develop Rational Optimism	98

Discover Your Authentic Potential	100
Find Wisdom to Make a Decision	102
Understand Financial Decisions	104
Know the True Intentions of Others	106
See Beyond Fear	108
Stop Negative Thoughts	110
Improve Imagination When Creating	112
Improve Your Ability to Visualize	114
Achieve with Less Effort	116
Find Ideas for New Projects	118
Convey Love to One in Need	120
Find Relief from Melancholy	122
Bring Forgiveness	124
Uncover Honest Feelings	126
Experience Underlying Passion	128
Open the Emotions Within Attraction	130
Heal a Relationship Damaged by Betrayal	132
Improve Friendship	134
Protect with Love	136
Find Relief from Anxiety	138
Break the Cycle of Worry	140
Find Peace When Overwhelmed	142
Maintain Good Health	144
Prevent an Illness from Developing	146
Recover When Treatment is Underway	148
Restore Health When an Illness has Passed	150
Find New Depths of Energy	152
Protection from Negative Attachments	154
Reconnect with Your Soul	156
Find Peace When There is Disruption	158
Ease Self-Destructive Behavior	160
Turn Loneliness into Connection	162
Find Affinity with an Enemy	164
Discover Limiting Flaws	166
End a Period of Misfortune	168
Strengthen Personal Confidence	170
Strengthen Willpower Over Temptation	172
Improve Leadership Abilities	174
Endure Stasis in Peace	176

Increase the Momentum of Your Efforts	178
Clear Dark Energies from a Location	180
Protect Against Energy Thieves	182
Attract Help When in Need	184
Dismiss the Will of an Enemy	186
Inspire Strangers to Admire You	188
Make the Unwanted Stay Away	190
Speaking the Words of Power	193
The Origin of The Words	197
The Future of Magick	199
Exploring Magick	201

Introduction: The Mystical Adventure

Imagine using magick without any aim, desire or hope, without trying to solve problems, and seeking no gain. Imagine if this magick started to bring you all the things you want, and solved your problems. What if it increased your peace, passion, understanding, and your purpose in life? That's only the beginning of what this book can do for you.

The second part of this text is like a complete book in itself, with the most powerful sigils for creating change in your world.

In all the other books we have published, you get to use magick in a straightforward way, where you choose a problem or desire and target your magick directly. You might have a particular outcome that you want or a problem you want to solve, so you choose the appropriate magick. With Part One of this book you aim for nothing, but get more than you could imagine. With Part Two, you can direct the magick where you want. This combined power, to direct your magick while letting the larger mysteries guide your life, is one of the most enjoyable and effective ways to bring healing, strength, certainty and creative control to all that you do.

On the first page of a magick book it is common practice to make a long list of claims about what's possible, from earning money, to healing, influencing others, or whatever it is the readers might be looking for. This book is different because the powers are a gentle way of empowering your connection to your heart, soul, and mind. And, the benefits are too many to list on a single page. Using the method in Part One, people have found healing, a calming of the mind, new energy, and enthusiasm for life, but the scope of the magick is too wide to summarize. In Part Two, the rituals are the most potent form of magick created using the successful *Words of Power* Method.

Mystical Words of Power uses a magickal method that requires only your thoughts and feelings, your voice, and the images in the book. It's as easy as magick gets.

The two parts of the book seem so different that they could have been published as separate books, but the underlying power is connected, and they complement each other directly. You get the most out of using both. I don't think I should say too much more before letting you discover the magick. What I will say is that, although you could dive into the results-based rituals of Part Two straight away, because you need a result right now, it's not the best way. For one thing, the basic techniques and ideas are all described in Part One, so if you skip ahead, you might not have all the information for Part Two.

Also, I strongly suggest that you use at least one of the rituals in Part One, before trying anything else. It will help more than you think. This book is called *Mystical Words of Power* because there is more to this than just getting results, and if you want those results, allowing some of that mystical power into your life is the best way to empower the rest of your magick.

Part One: The Mystical Words

The rituals in Part One encourage a mystical connection to reality. This connection, strange as it sounds, enables your life to improve effortlessly. The magick is connected to your deepest desires, and works with high Angelic powers to guide your life according to your genuine needs.

There are seven rituals covering Perception, Knowledge, Imagination, Love, Healing, Transformation, and The Empowered Mind. This might sound abstract, so I'll say that all these rituals are filled with immense compassion, and will give you the feeling that you are being looked after, guided, nurtured, and protected. For some people, this feeling alone will make the magick worthwhile. It can be a really beautiful experience.

If you practice these rituals as described, you might find hundreds of problems solving themselves, desires falling into place, and your path through life becoming easier with more opportunities for success. These are all pretty big claims, but for anybody who has used *Words of Power* or *The Greater Words of Power*, you will know there is boundless potential in this magick.

There is, unsurprisingly, also a more mystical aspect to what happens within the rituals and in your life. Many of the rituals encourage you to experience the world in a mystical way, that can range from improved intuition and insight to visions and psychic abilities.

If these rituals are so powerful and effortless, why is there a need for any other magick? From the way I'm talking it sounds like this magick makes everything else redundant, and you can forget about the rest of occultism. If we're honest, this all sounds too good to be true, so let me clarify that this is a mystical process first and foremost, and remember that I said you don't aim for results. You perform the magick for the sake of the experience, and the results come almost as a side-effect.

I want to make it clear in these early pages, which you will hopefully read for free before you buy the book, that while the claims I make are genuine, this isn't an instant and permanent solution to everything. That would be outrageous. I know it sounds like you'd never need to put in any effort or use any other magick, but that's not the case. There's a reason this book has the word 'mystical' in the title. There is a mystery here, a personal mystery, and it is not as simple as sitting back and watching your life become perfect.

Life is not static, frozen or locked. You are a part of the fluidity of your life, with the choice to shape your fate rather than have it happen to you, and no matter how magick helps, your freedom to interact with life means your responses affect your reality. The way you respond to any circumstance changes a million tiny details that subsequently shape your life in a new way. Every time something happens, you react, respond, feel something or do something, and you cause change. Often, that's perfect, but sometimes problems arise, with new challenges or a cascade of changes that you can't keep up with.

Even when your life is being helped by magick, there is always the potential for you to respond in ways that bring minor chaos and confusion, or emotional problems that you don't even know are there until it's almost too late. So, life will continue to have its ups and downs, but I sincerely believe every one of them will be instructive, and every one of them will be easier to solve.

The rituals in this book are worth doing for their own sake, for the insight and experience they give you, for the mystical experiences that you may feel, and that's such an important point that it's tempting to repeat it a hundred times, but I promise I won't. And as well as that, I believe that doing these rituals gives you a strong foundation, where Angelic power is always there for you; always supporting and guiding you to make the best decisions, to avoid the worst accidents and mistakes, to attract the best circumstances and opportunities. You will still ponder your decisions, work hard to create your life, and maybe even work magick to get the results you want, but this book will give you the strongest foundation from which to work without struggle.

The magick doesn't cure your life of all challenges, mysteries, and intrigue. It doesn't take away all the surprises, and it doesn't make you immune to life itself. If it did, life would be boring, and this magick would be a mistake. But it takes away so much of the battle and makes way for you to shape your life creatively. I believe that using these rituals will help you to live an enjoyable and meaningful life, and in many cases, life will just become better, without you even trying. Sometimes, just like with normal life, your efforts will make the real difference, but the magick will still be there to make things easier.

You are inviting the power of Angels and Archangels to bring great power, healing, and guidance to many areas of your life, providing an overall change that is enormously beneficial to you from the moment you begin. But life is filled with change and challenge, and it is how you respond to your changing desires and circumstances that really counts.

Despite this slightly weird explanation, the magick itself is easy. The method involves looking at sigils, which contain Divine words and Angelic names, and speaking those names while performing exercises in perception or thought. It can appear so simple that you might think it's too good to be true, too easy. It might look like New Age wishful thinking or something too obscure to be real. I hope you can see past that, and discover that the method, despite its apparent simplicity, was arrived at by distilling and purifying the essence of many magickal secrets into something workable.

It might look like there's a lot to read and learn, but it's easier than you'd think, and in a couple of hours you'll know everything you need to know. In my youth I passed many difficult months where I spent hours performing intensive rituals every day. Magick used to be opaque and inaccessible; it could take you a year to find out that something was a waste of time. I hope you can see the beauty of being able to try this magick in a short time from now.

At some points in the book, it might sound like I'm repeating myself, but I keep this to a minimum, and when I do, it isn't for emphasis or because I think the point needs drumming home. This repetition always contains some variation, and makes sure a point is made in several different ways, in different contexts. That means every word counts. You don't have to study this furiously, making sure you never miss a word, but everything is here for a reason.

If you're new to magick, this is a good way to explore how it can work, and it will give your future magick greater strength. And if you are experienced with the occult, I'm sure you'll see how this method can provide a direct shift in reality, to make your dreams and desires ease into place.

And remember, this magick is a beautiful experience, and that is where you begin. Seeking the experience of the magick, but at the same time knowing that you may not experience much at all, at first. This might sound like a contradiction, but it means you don't perform one ritual and expect the heavens to deliver a mystical experience. It means you treat every ritual as valid, and allow the mysteries and powers to unfold as they will.

The Method

The magick in this book is based on the method found in the other *Words of Power* books. The catch with Part One is that you have to do it for its own sake, for the enjoyment of the spiritual journey, for the experience of the magick, and not to seek the results that may come. This might sound a bit too mystical, and may even sound impossible, but when you try the magick, you'll see it's very easy to do.

Now, I have to admit there is a bit of a contradiction here. For each of the seven rituals, I list all the possible powers. And it's true that being aware of these powers helps; otherwise I wouldn't list them. Knowing what they are is good, but let it be a form of knowing rather than a desire for a specific result. The genius of this system is that it reaches into your deepest needs and creates, adjusts, or attracts the results you need most at any given time.

You don't have to put in masses of effort into choosing rituals or avoiding 'lust for result,' which is how magick usually works. Here, you do the magick and get on with your life. And then you find that the results I've talked about are like a side effect. They happen when they do.

But who wants to go on a spiritual journey? Who wants to do magick without a goal? Not many people, from what I've seen and heard. People like the *idea*, but not the practice, because it sounds like hard work. It's much more exciting to do a money ritual and get some instant cash. I understand that, completely, but you might find that this is magick that can be immensely practical for you. It's easy to do, takes very little time, with no equipment at all, and it can be truly transformative.

Even if you've no interest in going on a spiritual quest I know that if you perform the magick, you will experience changes that you will never regret.

You may look at me, and my books, and wonder what right do I have to tell you how to explore spirituality. Although I've written books about inner magick and working with Archangels, I'm also a man who's written books about sex magick, influence, and riches. How can I be the person to guide you on a spiritual quest?

The truth is I have no special authority or power granted to me, but I have knowledge, experience, and many decades spent working with people who have used magick. I am not claiming to have great spiritual wisdom, and I am not your guide. But I have good magickal methods that you are free to use to find the guidance that arises from within you.

What I share here is the combined work of many people that I have known. And as for those books I've written, about money, sex, and other material desires, I make no excuses. We are humans with material desires, and I believe that using magick to fulfill those desires is one of the fastest ways to increase your spirituality. It's far too simplistic to think that material desires are unspiritual. Part of our quest is to be spiritual beings in a material existence.

There is nothing noble or spiritual about struggling and suffering. When you struggle to achieve anything, or when you struggle to affect the real world, you don't feel as though you are part of the world or in tune with the universe. When you use magick to make life easier and get what you want, you become in tune with the universe, and *less* attached to material goods. You become far more in tune with your spiritual power. The more you get in the material world, the less interested you are in the material world, and then you find yourself becoming more spiritual without even trying.

It's almost impossible even to say what 'spiritual' means, but I will say there is nothing unspiritual about indulging in the pleasures. I loathe greed, and I often work to make things fair for those who are struggling (especially artists), but I openly admit that I like having money, using money, and living a full and sensual life.

As you will discover in these pages, 'spiritual' in this book doesn't mean rejecting the world, living a meager life while looking to the heavens at the expense of pleasure. It is about embracing the world and the place you choose to be in the world, and living a life of pleasure. It's about experiencing reality rather than avoidance. Your pleasure is a vital part of the magick. The uplifting of the spirit that then occurs is beautiful and true.

In this first part of the book, there are no goals, but many adventures, journeys, and opportunities.

The Pleasure

Magick should never become something you feel you are obliged to do. It's meant to be a pleasure in itself. If you read the book now and think it's not for you, put it aside, and know that some time in your long life you may find this is exactly what you want. It might be in a moment of need, spiritual crisis, to help with other magick, or merely from a curious sense that the time is right. But if you don't feel ready for it yet, don't force yourself. If you feel any curiosity at all, you might find some pleasant surprises when you try the magick.

At the same time, this magick works best when you go in with some sense of commitment. If you try the rituals and one week later nothing has happened, don't be too surprised. Some people get instant results, but others don't feel anything or notice anything for weeks, so you should be willing to have some patience. If you are looking for results, you're doing this the wrong way around. The magick should be a pleasant exploration and experience, and what comes into your reality is a bonus. (Don't forget, Part Two is there for results!)

Some readers of my books get frustrated because they read reviews or stories where people describe getting great results on day one, and powerful sensations of Angels within seconds, and then they think it *has* to be that way. It doesn't. You may feel little or nothing for quite some time. With this magick, you will eventually feel something, and you'll probably have many profound experiences. But it might not be immediate. And you have to go into it knowing that it doesn't matter.

So, I suggest you go into this the same way you would when you take on any large project. When you join a gym or start a fitness regime, you should not be checking your weight every day. You commit to losing weight and just get on with it. Losing weight, becoming fit, building muscle; it all takes time, even though the changes begin on the first day that you struggle away on the treadmill. Eventually, there is no struggle at all, and it becomes pleasant to be there. It's the same with this magick, in that the changes are there instantly, and a great deal will be set in motion from the moment you begin, even if it takes time for you to see how those changes are eventuating.

Starting this magick is not as difficult as starting a fitness regime on a treadmill. This magick is far more enjoyable, but it may be similar in that you won't notice the changes for some time, even though they are underway.

The trick is to find a blend of commitment and ease, making sure you don't perform the magick out of obligation. As with many aspects of the occult there is a slight contradiction here, but that's the nature of mysticism. The secret is to *enjoy* the rituals for their own sake, while you perform them. If at any point you don't enjoy them or become frustrated, stop for a while. But because you have made a commitment, come back to them at a later time. You might wake up the next day, or maybe a few weeks later, knowing it's the right time to carry on.

For a lot of people, the immediate sensations of this magick will be intense. You can feel a rush of Angelic power and sense the full potential of the energy within these workings, but I don't want you to need or expect that. Know that your own experience is valid, and if nothing happens, that's actually an illusion; it just means things are happening beneath the surface for now.

The results and benefits I've talked about; they might come instantly. I've seen people move away from depressive moods, overcome emotional pain, and be restored after great trauma, all with astonishing speed. But for other people, it takes a long time. Accept that it might be instant, or that it might not, or it might happen in bits, here and there, with long periods where not much seems to be happening.

I often talk about the need for patience in magick even though, as has been noted, many of the rituals work well for impatient people because they bring the things you want in life much faster. The same is true here. Things may change rapidly, or the benefits and changes may come slowly. All that matters is doing the magick for its own sake. If you can't think why you'd ever want to make such a commitment, read the rest of the book, see what's within those rituals and see if it stirs some desire to be a part of this magickal experience.

Overall, I would say that Part One is not for the impatient who seek an instant change. If you are willing to see what happens, however impressive or slight it may be, I know you will eventually look back and feel that it took no time at all for great changes to occur.

I also know that for most people, it's unusual to perform these rituals without feeling *something* change. There can be visions, moments of Angelic contact, insight, and emotions that are compelling and beautiful. Sometimes, a day later, when you least expect it, when the magick is far from your mind, there will be an ordinary moment that becomes magickal. This can be extremely moving and makes you feel like you are integrated into your chosen reality, not just being dragged along by random events.

You should also know that when you do this sort of magick, it can put you in a powerful place and can open you up to personal development. That is, an improvement in your life can make room for old wounds to arise. This doesn't mean the magick is disruptive or unpleasant in any way, but that when you are strong enough, emotions may arise because you now have the power to deal with them easily. Only when you are ready will this happen, and nothing will ever happen that you aren't able to cope with. Don't worry that performing this magick opens up a flood of negativity for you to deal with. It's the opposite. What it means is that inner damage or pain that's harmed you will get the easiest possibility to emerge and be released, bringing a level of inner healing you could rarely hope for.

Also, as life improves, it's easier to deal with problems you've avoided for a long time. You might find you have the strength to tackle problems you've avoided, emotions you've denied, and situations that once terrified you, all without it feeling like a challenge.

Everything is in flux, and you aren't just a passenger in life. The magick in this book will provide immense relief and guidance, but your life won't just stop changing or become predictable. It's more likely that you will be led to discover who you really are, what you want, and how to get it, without the need to struggle for your desires.

Expect nothing and allow everything and I believe you will find this magick to be one of the greatest adventures.

The Changes

This magick is based on the same essential method found in *Words of Power* and *The Greater Words of Power*, but there are some differences which may be of interest. There is no need to explain every change. Many readers won't know the other books, and if you *are* familiar with them, you will readily see how the method differs as you work through the book.

There are a few details that *are* worth addressing, however, whether you are familiar with the books or not.

The first is the shape of the sigils. Sigils are often made up of lines, circles, and celestial alphabets. Often, they contain Hebrew letters. In the *Words of Power* method, the Divine words and Angelic names are written in Hebrew because (whatever your beliefs or background) these letters form a powerful connection to the energy you seek to employ. In the first two books, the words were arranged in a rectangular box. In this book, they are arranged within a circle.

The words could be arranged without anything other than a simple line drawn around them, and the presentation is not overly important, whether it's a box or a circle. But using a circle in this book is not just a gimmick, because we have found that certain shapes not only evoke particular emotions and ways of seeing but also assist with scanning the letters in a slightly different way. You will see how this works when we get to the actual scanning method, but the circular shape helps with the way your eyes absorb the image of the letters.

The circle is also used because in this version of the ritual, *The 42 Letter Name of God* encircles the entire sigil. In the original *Words of Power*, this Name was used only to attune you to the Hebrew letters, but here it is present in every ritual.

In Part One there is *The Attuning Ritual*, which is used to connect with the magick of the sigils. This is a different version of *The Activating Ritual*, which you may know from the other *Words of Power* books. Even if you never use the rituals in Part One, you will need to use *The Attuning Ritual* before moving on to Part Two.

You'll notice that the sigils contain circular pentagrams, split into light and dark. These were square in the original books. Again, the slight change is only to help with the scanning process. You don't need to look at these pentagrams directly, but their presence affects the ritual on a subconscious level. If you have any fear regarding the pentagram, please read about its sacred history which has nothing to do with evil. Here it helps to make reality more open to change.

To be clear, these sigils could be set out exactly as they were in the first books, and they would still work. But we were guided to this method and found that for the mystical approach to this magick, the circular shape makes the magickal process easier.

In Part One of the book, there are only seven sigils. These sigils are designed for the mystical and spiritual connection I talked about earlier, so you don't need fifty or a hundred. You only need seven sigils, because each contains the potential to access hundreds of ways to change, modify, and improve yourself and your circumstances. (For more targeted magick, Part Two has over fifty sigils for specific situations.)

The method remains so easy you can do it while sitting on a park bench, without anybody knowing you are performing magick. It's better if you perform it in a place where you can say the words out loud, although many people have found that just hearing the words in their head works well. I recommend using the complete method, where the words are spoken, but if you can't for reasons of privacy, you can still get results.

How this Magick Works

If you were to describe the magick in any *Words of Power* book to a stranger, you might say, 'You just look at a list of words and names and then say them out loud, while thinking about what you want to change.' That's not entirely accurate, but does give you an idea of its simplicity.

To add a little more detail, I will say that you scan over the words with your eyes and vocalize the sounds, while engaging in slight mental or emotional shifts. By viewing the letters, and calling these words and names in the order shown, you are able to convey your desire to the Angels. The Angels will understand your need because of how you feel, and it is their sacred duty to respond. The magick is safe because each ritual contains words that enshrine the working with Divine protection and power. But even with that detail you might wonder how looking at names and saying them out loud can possibly work.

I don't want to spend time discussing theory, because working with magick and feeling something change, or having a result come about, just once, will tell you more about magick than any big ideas, speculations, or opinions. And there are millions of opinions. I'll only give you a basic overview of why this is a plausible magickal technology.

First of all, a lot of the power comes from the use of Hebrew letters to make contact with the powers and spirits. Some readers are concerned that without a Western or Judeo-Christian background, the magick won't work, or won't mesh with their own beliefs. We've found the magick even works for atheists, and people from all other religions that we know about. Why this is the case is open for debate. In some mystery traditions, and religions, it's believed that the letters are sacred, but others think it's more to do with repeated use of the letters in a magickal way. Whatever the truth, the letters are a powerful key that makes contact with the spirits and energies much stronger than if the words were written in any other alphabet.

You don't have to know Hebrew, because each word is written out phonetically, so it's not a problem. You don't even need to know what the words mean, except that you are calling on Divine powers and

Angelic beings to assist you. (If you want to know what the words mean, see The Origin of the Words at the end of the book.)

Why, though, does having a list of Divine words and Angelic names do anything? We were fortunate to be led to a manuscript that explains how the specific ordering of these names can unlock powers that are conveyed by these Angels and Archangels. The most important aspect of this is that Angels always work in certain ranks and hierarchies, so when you use this ordering method, the Angels are instructed to work with other Angels. This means a small sigil with just a few words can be used to call on a large number of associated Angels, precisely calling on the aspect of the Angel that can help with the exact situation you want to approach. Instead of writing out hundreds of Angel names in the hope of covering all the bases, the coded ordering allows you to list just a few names and access hundreds of Angelic powers.

It was announced in early 2019 that The Gallery of Magick will continue as a magickal order in private, but that our last few books will be published before the end of 2021, and then we will retreat from the world of writing and publishing. The final book will explain the origin of this ordering technique and its method. It is not straightforward and contains layers of deep mystery, but if you are curious about the workings of magick, you will eventually be given all the secrets. For the practical magick in this book it makes no difference, except that while working the magick, it may help you understand why you often feel a host of compassionate entities are helping you.

Why is *The 42 Letter Name of God* used in these rituals? The short answer is that it helps to trigger the rest of the magick, for reasons too theoretical to get into in a short book. Fragments of the Name are also included in some of the sigils, as Divine words, for the power they bring.

The 42 Letter Name of God is often thought to be derived from the *Ana b'Koach* prayer. It's true that if you take the first letter from each word of the prayer, that gives you *The 42 Letter Name of God*. But only if you ignore the last line. If you study the prayer, you'll see it has 49 words, which means it is clumsy thinking to believe this is the source of the Name. It is most likely that the prayer only reflects and presents the Name.

I believe, as many scholars have pointed out, that *The 42 Letter Name of God* has more hidden origins, which remain difficult to discern and are the subject of much debate. The *Ana b'Koach* prayer is not the origin so much as a way of hiding the letters in plain sight, and using them to create a prayer for those who like that sort of thing. Some people believe that using this prayer in conjunction with *Words of Power* is a good option, and although I'd never say you should avoid it, I don't think it's in any way required because the letters of the Name are already used in a magickal way. You see and speak *The 42 Letter Name of God* in *The Attuning Ritual*. (You do this in sections, so it's easy to do.)

If you already know much about *The 42 Letter Name of God* you will be aware that some of the letters are interchangeable with near-identical letters. This is almost the same as writing **The** instead of **the**, and doesn't stop the Name from being the Name. God is God, whatever language you use. The letters are obviously important, in magickal terms, but I will not go into the details here because most people won't care. I am letting you know so that if you find other versions of the letters, you won't assume something is wrong. The version we have chosen is the most effective for magick, with pronunciations based on vowel markings found in various magickal sources.

All that matters for you is that the Name brings power to the magick, regardless of your background or your beliefs about religion or the occult.

Some people still don't like the idea that they might be saying something they don't understand, and they wonder why all these Angel names aren't found in standard Angelic dictionaries. If you want to know what it all means and what you're saying, see the later chapter on *The Origin of The Words*, which should give you enough information.

To work the magick, you only need to know that you are connecting your inner desires to the power of Angels and Archangels, and it is their purpose to help you fulfill your chosen destiny.

Some people fear that payment or sacrifice is required in order to receive results, or that magick will cause a karmic backlash to even things out. Such fears are based on superstition. With this magick, your gratitude is all that's required, and there is never any form of backlash. Magick is safe, but it does bring change, so be willing to accept the changes and experiences you ask for.

Magick sometimes works instantly, because everything is aligned and you are ready for the changes you request. Sometimes it takes longer because you are asking for major changes. It's often surprising how it works out. Problems that seem enormous can shift easily, while small issues can be more stubborn, and you're often led to see something else that's the real underlying problem.

By using the magick in this section, Part One, you will experience a mix of insight and wisdom, and you may find that in time everything works out the way you want. Or, if you find the magick offers you more clarity regarding your problems and the changes you need, you can use the rituals in Part Two to influence the reality of your world directly. Although I have said that previously, I am making the point here that using Part Two is more effective if your work is guided by the wisdom, knowledge, emotions, or visions you experience when using Part One. But how you use the magick is up to you, and I trust that with a brief experience of the rituals you will work out the best way to integrate this magick into your life.

The Attuning Ritual

This ritual should be performed once only, to allow the imagery of the sigils to become a part of your magickal work. You are attuning yourself to the magick, and taking the letters and images within.

Even if you have used *Words of Power* or *The Greater Words of Power*, I strongly recommend performing this ritual. It is so short that it may feel like nothing has happened, or there was no reason to do it, but the procedure is an important step in getting this magick to work.

The ritual makes use of the letters found in *The 42 Letter Name of God,* which are split into seven words. These are not ordinary words. In some cases, a translation is possible, as with Karasatan, which can be translated as 'To Tear Away Satan', but even this is disputed by those who say that the words are only vocalizations that enable you to speak the entire *Name of God*. Here, the words are represented as follows, with the pronunciation beneath in parentheses.

Avigehitotzi
(AH-VEE-GEH-EE-TAW-TSEE)

Karasatan
(KAH-RAH-SAH-TAHN)

Nagidahikaysha
(NAH-GEE-DAH-EE-KAY-SHAH)

Bitarotzatag
(BEE-TAH-RAW-TZAH-TAHG)

Chekevatinei
(CHEK-EH-VAH-TIN-UH-EE)

Yagalipehzekei
(YAH-GAH-LEE-PEH-ZEH-KAY)

Shukovatzoiaht
(SHOO-CAW-VAH-TS-AWE-EE-AHT)

There are many ways to interpret the pronunciation of these words, and it differs from book to book. This magick is Pronunciation Proof, but if you need help, check the chapter called *Speaking the Words of Power* at the end of the book.

To begin the ritual, try to be alone, where your focus can settle gently on the magick. Know that you are beginning a magickal process, and let your gaze rest on the white circle in the center of the sigil. You do not stare at it, but let your eyes remain there while being aware of the other shapes and letters. You may find that your eyes wander, and that the other shapes and letters may distort or fade in and out of view. Keep bringing your gaze back to the white circle, gently, with minimal effort, and know that in doing this the images of magick are becoming a part of you.

After about a minute you begin to scan the letters in the outer circle. Scanning is not the same as reading, because all you do is look at the shapes of the letters, not trying to read or understand. You are only looking at the letters briefly. You start at the very top of the circle and scan your eyes anti-clockwise. When you get to the bottom of the circle, you will be looking at inverted letters, and that's fine. When you get to the top, stop, and speak the first Word which is Avigehitotzi, pronounced as AH-VEE-GEH-EE-TAW-TSEE. The words are all listed under the sigil to make this easy. Don't worry about being too accurate with the letter scanning or the pronunciation. You do not have to get this perfectly right, and doing it in a relaxed manner is far more productive than worrying about getting it right.

Now scan your eyes over the letters again, starting at the top, moving anti-clockwise until the circle is complete, and speak the second word in the list. You repeat this seven times, once for each word. By the end, you will have scanned the circle seven times, and spoken all seven words. After the final word has been spoken, the ritual is over without any need for a closing gesture or ceremony. As soon as it's done, you're ready for the rest of the magick, and remember, it only needs to be performed once.

People worry about getting this right and feel a sense of panic if they miss a word or make a mistake. If you feel like it went wrong, repeat it when you're feeling calmer, but know that this is a gentle attuning, and if you are relaxed, it will work. There's no harm in performing it more than once, but just once, ever, will be enough. The sigil appears on the following page.

AH-VEE-GEH-EE-TAW-TSEE

KAH-RAH-SAH-TAHN

NAH-GEE-DAH-EE-KAY-SHAH

BEE-TAH-RAW-TZAH-TAHG

CHEK-EH-VAH-TIN-UH-EE

YAH-GAH-LEE-PEH-ZEH-KAY

SHOO-CAW-VAH-TS-AWE-EE-AHT

The Practice of Magick

The ritual process for Part One is described in this chapter. If you want to use Part Two first, you can, but please read this because it gives you a guide to some of the core techniques.

Make sure you have performed *The Attuning Ritual* from the previous chapter. You can begin your first ritual moments after *The Attuning Ritual*, or weeks later.

Choose which of the seven rituals you will be working with. You *can* perform several rituals in a single day, but I recommend using only one of these rituals a day until you are familiar with them. After that, you may wish to perform them often or occasionally, and learning how to choose the best approach to this will be discussed later. For now, I will focus on performing a single ritual to explain the technique. I will use the example of the first ritual; *The Ritual of Perception*.

1. To begin a ritual, find a time and place where you can be alone for a few minutes. Being surrounded by distractions, or having people interrupt you, will not work. You can perform the ritual anywhere you like, at any time of day or night, but if you can find the privacy to perform the ritual with full concentration and an ability to say the words out loud, that is perfect.

Ensure you have read everything that comes before this section. You can work with the sigils in the eBook or the paperback, and the results will be the same. It is your perception of the sigils that matters, not how they are displayed.

2. Turn to the page of your chosen ritual. Spend some time reading about the nature of the ritual and the potential results. If this generates feelings of excitement or expectation, that is fine for now, even though you will let go of expectation during the ritual itself. You should read this section every time you perform the ritual because each time that you do, you may get new insights into how these powers might work for you. Never let it become boring or a task. This is a moment where you understand and feel the potential of the ritual. Try to sense the scope of the ritual and how much change it is capable of bringing to your life.

3. Turn to the page with the sigil. Scan the outer circle of letters in the sigil three times, anti-clockwise. This is the same technique used in *The Attuning Ritual*, where you allow yourself to see the shape of the letters, without any particular thoughts, as you guide your eyes around the circle, anti-clockwise, three times. You do not need to say anything.

As you do this, let go of all expectation. You are performing the ritual for the sake of the experience, and you let your expectations about what may happen fall away. (If you find this impossible, don't worry; it is the act of allowing expectations to fall away that matters more than how good you are at allowing. Be easy with yourself, and know that the intention to let go of expectation is enough.)

4. Now gaze at the whole sigil, with your focus on the white space and the outer black circles. Your attention is not on the words. You don't avoid looking at the words, but you let your gaze rest on the white space and outer circles, so the letters can be absorbed into your subconscious, and the sigil is drawn within you. This only needs to take ten seconds or so, and never more than a minute.

5. You now perform the Associated Action. This is a brief moment where you recall a moment from your past, and imagine a moment in the future. It doesn't have to be an important or interesting moment that you recall, and it doesn't even have to be real, which makes it really easy. You can think back to a time in your life and remember the light glittering on the surface of a lake, or the breeze moving leaves in the street, or somebody's smile.

It can be any moment and doesn't need to be emotional or beautiful. It only needs to feel like a memory, even if you're making it up. In the past, I believed that real memories were vital to the process, but found that it became distracting trying to recall real events. Experimentation showed that invented memories work just as well, so long as they feel like the past. I find it much easier to pick a year, a season, a place and imagine what I might have seen, heard or experienced. Allow yourself to experience this 'memory' for a brief moment.

Now you imagine a moment from your future. Imagine being somewhere, anywhere, a year or so from now, and imagine seeing, hearing, or experiencing something. It can be absolutely anything so long as it is not the same image as your first 'memory.' It should also be something plausible, and not a goal. Don't picture yourself dating a celebrity. Just imagine something ordinary from the near future. Again, I often pick a random place and season, and imagine whatever comes to mind. It can be as mundane as a car driving past.

Sometimes, these moments are almost like visions and can be quite strange, but usually you picture something and imagine that it's going to happen. This Associated Action might seem a bit strange, but it's a way of loosening your reality a little more. It's a vital part of this process. The sigil should still be in front of you, but you don't have to look at it while doing this, and can even close your eyes.

6. Now scan each Hebrew word of the sigil. Scanning means that you move your eyes from right to left, which is the opposite to reading English.

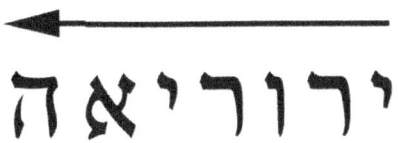

You are not trying to read, only to look at the letter shapes. If your eyes wander back and forth a little, that is fine. You let your eyes settle on each letter, but you don't have to stare. The entire scan of a word won't take more than a few seconds, at most. When you have scanned a word, you then move down to scan the next word and continue working down the sigil, scanning each word from right to left.

You don't need to think, feel, or expect anything during this part of the ritual. When you have scanned all the Words of Power, briefly recall what the ritual is about. I find the easiest way to do this is to think of the name of the ritual. Here, I would think *The Ritual of Perception*, and that would give me a momentary reminder of everything I was thinking earlier as I pondered the descriptive notes.

7. You now speak the Words of Power which are printed beneath the sigil. There is one complete word on each line. All the sigils in this book

have the same two words at the beginning. Each word is made of several sounds.

These words are read as though they are English, from left to right. Read each word, just once, without trying to feel or expect anything.

Remember that every word is a Divine word or a connection to a spirit that works the will of the Divine. Each time you say a word, speak *as though you are being heard by the spirits*. You may experience sensations of Angelic contact, and if you do, notice them but continue with the ritual. If you feel nothing, that is to be expected most of the time.

Between each spoken word, glance up at the sigil. You do not need to look at a particular word, but glance at the sigil for a moment, and then speak the next word.

If you can, let the words vibrate through your throat as though you are breathing them out. You let them rumble up from your belly through the back of your throat, almost as though you are chanting or singing them. Think of the sounds as traveling to the ends of the universe because this makes it more powerful than muttering words in a quiet room.

This 'vibration,' where you let the words rumble out of you is not essential and will be impossible for many people. If need be, just say them out loud.

If you can't find the privacy even to say the words quietly, imagine hearing the words as though you are speaking them. Imagine speaking them loudly, so they reach the end of the universe.

Throughout this part of the ritual, you do not need to do anything except to make the sounds of the words and know that you are communicating your inner needs to countless Angels.

8. When the final word has been spoken, you end the ritual by closing the book, or looking up from it, and allow yourself to be present in this moment. Within the ritual you reached to the past and the future, so you seal the ritual by becoming aware of exactly where you are. This means nothing more than looking around the room, for example, and being aware of what you can see, hear, and feel. You are letting go of magick and coming back to your normal existence. After just a second or two of this, the ritual is complete.

What follows in the coming hours may be absolutely nothing, or there may be an immediate shift in your reality. Remember all that has been said in previous chapters, and see the upcoming chapters for more details on this point.

A Brief Summary

Use this summary only when you have completely understood the description above, and start by choosing a ritual.

1. Find a place where you can be alone with the book.

2. Read about the nature of the ritual and the potential results, and become aware of the change it is capable of bringing to your life.

3. Scan the outer circle of letters in the sigil three times, anti-clockwise, letting go of all expectation.

4. Gaze at the sigil, with your focus on the white space and the outer black circles.

5. Perform the Associated Action. Imagine a moment from your past, and then imagine a brief moment in your future.

6. Scan each Hebrew word of the sigil from right to left. When you have scanned them all, briefly recall what the ritual is about.

7. Speak the Words of Power that are beneath the sigil and know that you are communicating your inner needs to countless Angels.

8. Close the ritual by allowing yourself to be present in your current reality.

Receiving the Magick

Having read all that, you may have a lot of questions about how often to perform the magick, how it manifests, and what you're meant to do to get the most out of this system.

It's worth saying at this point that you don't need belief, conviction, or faith in the system. You only need to follow the instructions and then allow whatever happens to happen. It will help if you are slightly more self-aware than the average person. If you perform lots of rituals but then sit in front of a computer screen, with no room for your thoughts, you have less chance of sensing change, opportunity, or mystical moments.

Often, something spontaneous happens. You might feel a change, have something occur, or even experience a vision. The degree to which this happens can be anything from a small impression to something that leaves you quite stunned by the power of the Angels.

Guidance is another form of manifestation. You may find that through omens, coincidence, intuition, or just by somebody giving you unexpectedly good advice, you're guided to better things. But there are so many more ways, and I think it's best not to focus on this too much because you are meant to be performing the rituals for their own sake.

And let's not forget, there may not be a direct manifestation of a result because you are not seeking one. It may be that the spiritual practice of connecting to the powers of the rituals, has a spiritual effect on you that is gradual and almost unnoticed. If you look back some time from now and see how things have changed since day one, you will be amazed.

What if life seems to go wrong after a few days, or you have some kind of accident? Have you done something wrong? Are you being punished? I can't emphasize enough that you will never be punished or harmed by doing this magick. But just because the world is the way it is, some people will start the magick and a few days later something bad will happen. If you're nervous, it's easy to believe it's because of the magick. In reality, it could be that the magick has actually lessened the problem you encountered. Life is a mass of chaos, and sometimes we turn to magick when things feel like they about to go wrong, and even if you start using magick, your immediate problems have so much momentum they happen anyway. If so, reassure yourself that you now have magick on your side, which will help you recover and get back to normal.

Expect nothing, allow everything, and if something goes wrong all of a sudden, be brave enough not to blame the magick but know the magick can now protect you from the worst. It could be that you've encountered this magick just in time.

For most people, nothing dramatic will happen. But for some, things will start changing for the better very quickly. If you've turned to this style of magick at just the right time, when things are lining up in your life, when you're on the brink of change (whether you know it or not) you may find profound change occurring to you in seconds, hours, or days. Again, don't expect this, but if it happens, be prepared to enjoy whatever comes your way.

And remember to think of this whole practice in Part One as a worthwhile spiritual exercise for its own sake. Of course, that can be a challenge. It's like being asked to join a meditation center, or something similar, and being told not to expect change but that change will come. I admit, things like that can be frustrating to hear, and yet here I am saying the same thing. All I can say is *try the magick*. You'll enjoy it, and change will come, one way or another.

But how do you use this in an ongoing way? Is there a schedule to follow? There is not, and I am extremely reluctant to say that you should follow your instincts because I know many readers really want to be given a pattern to follow. If you want a pattern, there are several you could use.

You could, for example, perform one of the seven rituals each day, so that all seven are performed in a single week, and repeat this indefinitely.

An alternative would be to perform a single ritual once a day for a week, before moving onto the next ritual, so that after seven weeks you've had a good taste of all the magick.

Those are two patterns you *could* follow, but you might also find that doing magick every day isn't for you. Some people do one ritual, once a week or less, and some find that they like one or two of the rituals every now and then, and don't do the rest. This is all fine. You have a long life ahead of you, and the way you interact with this magick will be yours alone. Try it, see how it feels, and come up with your own schedule or pattern. The only thing I would warn against is doing too much. Trying to do all seven rituals every day is not a good idea. Stick to one ritual a day. If you want to add a ritual from Part Two that is fine, but otherwise, less is more.

There's no panic with Part One. You are not trying to get it right. You are only trying to get to know it. Welcome it into your life gently and see what happens.

You might also wonder if you need to give thanks or pay the Angels in some way. It's been said already that you don't need to pay for the experiences or make any type of sacrifice, but you are strongly encouraged to enjoy the results you seek. Usually, this means feeling a moment of gratitude when you get your result.

The magick is aimed so broadly, you may have many good things manifest in your life. As a result, you may not know what is caused by the magick and what isn't. Lots of good things will happen anyway, so you would be fooling yourself to believe the Angels were behind all positive changes.

The way to deal with this is to allow yourself to feel gratitude any time you feel there's something to be grateful for, but without directing it anywhere. You are not giving thanks to God or the Angels or anything else. You are only feeling grateful. It's a moment where you go, 'Ah, I'm so glad that happened,' without feeling the need to direct thanks anywhere else. If you have a separate practice in your life that involves giving thanks through prayer or meditation, that's fine, but you should also feel gratitude in the moments when something good happens.

At the same time, remember that your life is still going to have lots of texture, so when things appear to go wrong, don't think, 'Why would the Angels do this to me?' because they wouldn't. Recognize that it will pass and that greater powers are working beneath the surface, and that your problem is temporary. If you can, feel grateful that the situation will pass.

Gratitude has become such an industry in the past few decades, with whole books dedicated to gratitude journals, and the like. I know it can feel a bit like positive thinking, where you force yourself to see only the good while ignoring the bad. I'm not suggesting you do that. I think it's really important to feel the emotions that arise. When you feel anger or jealousy, experiencing those emotions allows them to tell you what you need to know. It is a vital part of our existence.

Habitual or ingrained emotions are less useful, such as when somebody becomes an 'angry person,' but when genuine emotions arise seemingly from nowhere, or in response to events and thoughts, it's fine to accept and pass through them.

I am not suggesting that gratitude takes the place of your rational and emotional self. All I suggest is that when you feel a moment of gratitude for something good that happens, no matter how small, you make it ten times more likely for the next good thing to happen. The Angelic powers exist to satisfy your needs, and if they see that you are grateful for the changes you experience they will continue to work as directed.

The magick will work to some extent even if you carry on without any gratitude at all, but becoming attuned to moments of change, to the pleasure of discovering something new, or obtaining something you want; feeling grateful in those moments is a fabulous way to make the magick more consistent and powerful.

The Angels are not responsible for everything good that happens, but whatever you do, never dismiss something good by thinking, 'That probably had nothing to do with magick. It was just a coincidence.' Coincidence is one of the most efficient ways for magick to work. A few coincidences may come together to bring you what you want. Magick works in many ways, and some of them may seem like small moments or tiny coincidences. Don't ignore or reject them, but see them as magickal structure working to bring you what you need. They are often a sign of more to come.

In Part One, remember you are not seeking anything, but you may still feel gratitude for the experience of the ritual, or for the sensations that follow, or indeed for any results that arise spontaneously. So, don't obsess over this, but keep it in mind as you progress through the magick.

The Ritual of Perception

This ritual connects you to your ability to perceive, by removing the shields that prevent clear perception and bringing clarity to the information you receive.

Perception is not only about the senses, but the way we interpret the senses. To perceive is not only to see or hear but to bring knowledge and understanding to what is gathered by the senses. The magnificent shortcuts our brain takes, to decipher and interpret all incoming data, are a blessing for mental efficiency, but one that comes with its problems. By perceiving the world through these shortcuts, we run the risk of missing out on what could be perceived. The habits of thought and perception filter out the new, the strange, the supernatural, and they prevent us from seeing the reality or potential of a moment or situation.

It would be exhausting and overwhelming to open the senses up so that all knowledge and associations were available at any one time. The flood of impressions from a single pebble would be too much to cope with. To perceive everything from its formation and history, down to its molecular structure, and its texture, color, mass, and position in the universe would be a waste of brainpower. *The Ritual of Perception* is not about making you open to *everything*, but making you open to *more*, both on a physical level and also in terms of interpretation.

To some extent it can be seen as a ritual that opens your eyes, and empowers all your senses, letting you perceive the beauty and truth of the universe, but also to see through any deception. It enables you to see things in a wider context and to determine the true reality of an object, person, or even something like a theory or an idea.

In performing this ritual, you unshackle some of your habitual perceptions, and you are given the power to sense and interpret the world with all the originality that makes you who you are. Your perception becomes integrated with your needs and purpose.

You will see things as they are and as they may be. You will see beauty where before you could not, but you will also see beneath surface beauty to perceive what is truly there. You may experience intuition in ways more physical and definite than ever before. If you give yourself space and time to be at peace you may even experience visions. These can range from deep insights into yourself, your life and your purpose, or into other people, and challenges you face. The visions you experience may be entirely mystical, leading you to discover more about the nature of reality, and your place in reality.

When your perceptions undergo this transformation, you may find greater clarity of mind, so you are able to understand people and ideas more easily.

The ability to perceive also enables you to impose your ideas and thoughts on the perceptions of others. You may find that people see you as more beautiful, innocent, or worthy of trust. It is possible to find that you can influence others to see you in the way of your choosing, making some people perceive you in one way, while others see you as something else. Your ability to communicate emotions, through speech and directly through willpower, will expand.

You will also sense the compassion of the universe, and in sensing it, you will find an inner strength that brings protection.

The Ritual Words of Perception

El is pronounced as ELL.

El Shaddai is pronounced as ELL-SHAD-EYE.

Pehzekei is pronounced as PEH-ZEH-KAY.

Iruraiah is pronounced as EE-ROO-RAH-EE-AH.

Yanevivael is pronounced as YAN-EV-EE-VAH-ELL.

Adoniyahu is pronounced as AH-DAW-NEE-AH-WHO.

Hayi is pronounced as HAH-YEE-EE.

The Perception Sigil

ELL
ELL-SHAD-EYE
PEH-ZEH-KAY
EE-ROO-RAH-EE-AH
YAN-EV-EE-VAH-ELL
AH-DAW-NEE-AH-WHO
HAH-YEE-EE

The Ritual of Knowledge

This ritual connects you to your memories and thoughts in a way that enables you to combine what you know into more refined knowledge.

Knowledge is more than the facts, opinions, and memories we have stored. Knowledge is the ability to combine what we know, to create awareness based on received information and an understanding of experience. Self-knowledge can be the key to creating a better life because in knowing who you are and what you need, your needs are more easily met, and frustrations fall away.

With the power of this ritual, you can gain an objective overview of reality, making it easier to make wise decisions, without being blinded by emotions or old opinions. You may find an ability to detach from basic thinking and look deeper. This can mean anything from becoming an original thinker, somebody who is inventive, or somebody who can begin to understand the workings of reality itself.

Following this ritual, you may find that you know more than you ever thought you knew. And you may find out more, not because you acquire facts, but because you gain intuition about truth. This may be anything from the truth about a particular person or situation, to the truth about reality and magick.

You may find that with your growing knowledge you are able to cope better with situations, rising above immediate concerns and able to laugh in a crisis. This is not because you are ignorant of the facts, but because your knowledge gives you sufficient perspective to see how reality works. You may develop optimism based not on wishes, but on knowledge of how those on a magickal path can be guided and protected.

In expanding your knowledge, you may sense the futures that await you, and this can assist you in choosing which of those you most want to pursue. Discovering your potential and the opportunities that you need to seek out to reach your potential, will lead to times of change, but your knowledge will enable you to make wise decisions.

With a better knowledge of yourself, and how you relate to others, you will cope better in difficult times and will find it easier to see what others mean when they speak.

You will understand the intentions of those close to you, as well as the decision makers who can affect your life. In financial matters, especially, you will gain a stronger understanding of what motivates other people who can help you, and what the best decisions are for your financial future.

You may develop the immense power to make timely decisions, with courage and conviction. And as new wishes arise, you will be able to see which are ephemeral, and which are connected to your true needs.

The Ritual Words of Knowledge

El is pronounced as ELL.

El Shaddai is pronounced as ELL-SHAD-EYE.

Tinei is pronounced as TIN-UH-EE.

Sehahsiah is pronounced as SEH-AH-SEE-AH.

Shameshiel is pronounced as SHAH-MEH-SHE-YELL.

Ihoazdiel is pronounced as EE-HAW-AH-ZED-EE-ELL.

Vesher is pronounced as VEH-SHAR.

The Knowledge Sigil

ELL
ELL-SHAD-EYE
TIN-UH-EE
SEH-AH-SEE-AH
SHAH-MEH-SHE-YELL
EE-HAW-AH-ZED-EE-ELL
VEH-SHAR

The Ritual of Imagination

This ritual connects you to the power of imagination, which can range from dreams and fantasies to images of strength that overcome fear.

Without imagination, we cannot create, and yet many people believe they have no imagination. If you decide to walk across the house to another room, that is an act of imagination; you thought of an alternate reality – you imagined it – and then you made it real by taking action. Imagination is much more than the ability to visualize or create, but in working this magick, you will develop skills that enable reality manipulation, as well as an improved ability to create or see images within your mind.

With your imagination strengthening, you often sense that you are free, but only within the confines of your current reality. Use your imagination to change your reality, by selecting an alternate future. This skill develops without effort, and you find yourself able to imagine and manifest new realities with ease. Without even understanding why, you may find that you are able to achieve more, with fortune appearing to be on your side, and with effort and strain removed from the equation.

If you are actively seeking new ideas, whether in your personal life, at work, or in relation to a creative project, the power of this ritual will bring the strongest energies of imagination to you, making it easy to imagine the ideas you seek.

When actively performing creative work, your ability to find inspiration will be improved. This applies to long-term projects, but also to events, such as a live performance, where you require additional inspiration in the moment.

If you have a poor visual imagination, it will not hold you back from being creative, but should you want to improve it, the energies of imagery will be made available to you. The energy of imagination can make this imagery as vivid as lucid dreams. It is no surprise that vivid dreams, and lucid dreams, may also occur when you perform this ritual.

Imagination also gives you strength, in that you are able to see beyond the obvious. It is an advanced form of perception, where you can imagine an alternative to the negative situation that you see before you. By picturing a different ending to your current story, you put yourself on the path to that reality.

If you are plagued by fear, there are few forces as strong as imagination to help you overcome it. Although it has been noted that an imagination running wild can be the source of fear and panic, an empowered imagination is able to see a better way. With imagination, you can remove fear by picturing the reality you want instead of the situation that worries you.

You may also find that many suppressed desires rise to the surface, as though your imagination is giving them a way to display themselves to you. Not all of these desires will be helpful, but you gain the opportunity to see which are the dreams that you want to accept.

The Ritual Words of Imagination

El is pronounced as ELL.

El Shaddai is pronounced as ELL-SHAD-EYE.

Bitaro is pronounced as BEE-TAH-RAW.

Bazraziah is pronounced as BAZZ-RAH-ZEE-AH.

Leoriel is pronounced as LEH-AWE-REE-YELL.

Iehonatiel is pronounced as EE-EH-AWE-NAH-TEE-ELL.

Lav is pronounced as LAHV.

The Imagination Sigil

ELL
ELL-SHAD-EYE
BEE-TAH-RAW
BAZZ-RAH-ZEE-AH
LEH-AWE-REE-YELL
EE-EH-AWE-NAH-TEE-ELL
LAHV

The Ritual of Love

This ritual connects you to the depths of your heart and enables you to sense feelings and emotions that may have long been subdued, while clarifying other emotions and removing old, unwanted sentiments that have been causing you harm. It will draw more love into your life.

You are loved and needed more than you know, and this ritual can help you sense the love that others have for you. It's possible to sense feelings from others directly, while in their presence, but also to gain a gradual awareness of how others feel.

You may also sense a mystical love that appears to come from reality itself. Many people find that they see beauty in unexpected places, and some can actually see the emotions between other people, visually. For others, it's less visual, but you gain a strong awareness not only of the feelings that relate to you but how other people are feeling. This empathic ability is under your control, and if ever you wish to turn it off, you only need to have that thought, and it will fade for a while. The feelings of so many people can be quite overwhelming, even if they are loving, so you have the option to let them ease away from your perception.

With the power of love obtained from this ritual, you may attract the forgiveness of those you have wronged. You may also find that you are finally able to forgive those you've been unable to forgive, and this brings great relief. When relationships have been damaged, you may find that any efforts to repair them are more successful than usual because the intensity of your love will be so palpable.

Your love will be more present, and you become less judgmental. People will sense your heart, meaning that when you feel compassion for another, they will feel comfort from you. The same power can help to relieve feelings of self-loathing or melancholy.

Many relationships improve in the aftermath of this ritual, although in some cases you may detect that somebody's feelings for you are not as loving as you wish them to be. When such awareness arises, you will feel the power to project your love to the other person, which will give them the opportunity to become more loving.

Projecting your love does not guarantee that everybody will want to be near you, and you may even find that some are resistant to the warmth of your heart at first. Give it time, and allow people to adjust as this magick develops. In some people, the changes are extreme and immediate, but in others, it can take time for the change to occur. Try to be patient with people as they adjust to you.

If you are attracted to somebody, or in a relationship, the power of love can help all those involved to sense the full potential of their hearts. Passion can be brought to the surface when it was never there, or if it faded a long time before.

The Ritual Words of Love

El is pronounced as ELL.

El Shaddai is pronounced as ELL-SHAD-EYE.

Avigeh is pronounced as AH-VEE-GEH.

Satsatekiah is pronounced as SAH-TSAH-TEH-KEE-AH.

Ladediel is pronounced as LAH-DEH-DEE-YELL.

Anafiel is pronounced as AH-NAH-FEE-ELL.

Yelah is pronounced as YEH-LAH.

The Love Sigil

ELL
ELL-SHAD-EYE
AH-VEE-GEH
SAH-TSAH-TEH-KEE-AH
LAH-DEH-DEE-YELL
AH-NAH-FEE-ELL
YEH-LAH

The Ritual of Healing

This ritual connects you to the underlying health that is within you. It should not be thought of as a cure for anything, and the disclaimer at the front of the book is important; magick is not medicine, and conventional treatments should be sought in all cases. But healing magick has a way of reminding the mind and body that they can reject some of the confusion that causes illness. This inner memory of health can help you maintain or regain a sense of wellbeing.

We are in a constant state of regeneration, and the mind and body work in harmony to restore balance and recover from illnesses. This ritual brings you into contact with a deep memory of your purest health, which you may feel as an immediate energy and vitality. People may notice that you appear younger or that your eyes are bright.

The mind and the body are intertwined in more ways than science used to imagine, but this reflects what has long been known to occultists, and this is why the mind can be helped by a healing ritual. Worry, torment, and other feelings of unease are likely to become less troubling. You feel them less in your body. Where fear may once have turned into a burning sensation in the stomach, you may find you are able to experience fear in a less distressing way. Fear remains a useful emotion, but it can be made to be protective rather than destructive and debilitating. In cases of cyclic anxiety, a sense of inner health can give you the strength to accept anxious feelings which in turn lets them pass. For some people, there will be a feeling of ongoing peace, as though the body has become settled, and this can help you to cope even during difficult times.

The power of inner health radiates from you and can have many effects beyond the body, such as shielding you from people who are a negative influence on your life.

Energy can improve, but as with all magick, the more you use a gift, the more you will get. Performing this ritual and remaining sedentary will not do much. If you improve your health and lifestyle, your health will improve without any magick, but if you add magick into the mix, then your small efforts to improve can be greatly amplified by Angelic power.

Ideally, the ritual will help you to maintain good health, but it is not a miracle cure, and even the most blessed life is patterned with periods of illness. Should you sense an illness taking hold, you might find the magick prevents it from developing as severely as it could. If you do become ill, you should recover more rapidly. And in cases where you need treatment, such as surgery, you can hope for a rapid restoration of health.

The Ritual Words of Healing

El is pronounced as ELL.

El Shaddai is pronounced as ELL-SHAD-EYE.

Itotzi is pronounced as EE-TAW-TSEE.

Qelileqaliah is pronounced as KELL-EE-LEK-AH-LEE-AH.

Michael is pronounced as MEEK-AH-ELL.

Adzariel is pronounced as ADD-ZAR-EE-ELL.

Mahash is pronounced as MAH-HAHSH.

The Healing Sigil

ELL
ELL-SHAD-EYE
EE-TAW-TSEE
KELL-EE-LEK-AH-LEE-AH
MEEK-AH-ELL
ADD-ZAR-EE-ELL
MAH-HAHSH

The Ritual of Transformation

This ritual connects you to the power to bring about change, both within yourself and in the world you experience.

When you ask people what they want they will often make a list of changes, but people are highly resistant to change. The illusion of comfort that you obtain by staying the same is tempting. This ritual works by making change something that happens easily. It helps you to see what needs to change both within yourself and in your world, and then offers insight into how you can make that change occur.

What people call soul-healing is catching a glimpse of your soul and obtaining a reminder of who you really are. The soul itself cannot be damaged and does not need healing, but sometimes your connection to your soul is hampered. This magick can warm and clarify the connection to your soul. It makes you more able to make transformation occur within your life.

In seeking transformation, you will be guided to discover the flaws that prevent you from being all that you want to be. Although this may be uncomfortable for a few moments, it is not a burden so much as a relief. The flaws may be far less problematic than you believe, and when you know who you are and what needs to be done, it is easier to accomplish everything you wish.

If you have self-destructive habits or behaviors, you may wish to treasure them and hold them close, for the comfort they appear to bring, but this ritual will make you see them as they are. It does not judge you or force you to live a pure life, but lets you see what may be self-destructive. As I have said, this book is not about living a small life, so don't worry that you will be forced to give up pleasure. If anything, this ritual may guide you away from minor pleasures so you can seek much grander indulgences.

When you experience a period of misfortune, the energy of transformation is the power you need to bring that misfortune to an end. Sometimes, a period of misfortune is caused by perceptions; things aren't any worse than usual, but your state of mind makes them appear so. In such cases, your state of mind will transform. Often, though, other forces, either internal or external, attract a series of events that make life difficult. It can feel like you are cursed, even when no such curse exists. Whatever the source of this ongoing misfortune, breaking the cycle will bring immense relief, and this ritual may bring that relief without you ever seeking the change directly. Sometimes you may only notice that a period of misfortune was real when it has passed. You may look back and see you were suffering unnecessarily.

All aspects of your life become open to change with this ritual, but it is especially potent when it comes to relationships, and can help a relationship to develop. For the lonely or isolated it can encourage your soul to reach out to others, making real-world connections to new friends a strong possibility.

If you feel any guilt about being in the world, which strange as it sounds is a remarkably common affliction, the transformation ritual can make you feel like you deserve the life you dream of having.

The Ritual Words of Transformation

El is pronounced as ELL.

El Shaddai is pronounced as ELL-SHAD-EYE.

Yagali is pronounced as YAH-GAH-LEE.

Iaheseiah is pronounced as EE-AH-EH-SEH-EE-AH.

Aniel is pronounced as AH-NEE-YELL.

Azariahu is pronounced as AZZ-ARE-EE-AH-WHO.

Reho is pronounced as REH-HAW.

The Transformation Sigil

ELL
ELL-SHAD-EYE
YAH-GAH-LEE
EE-AH-EH-SEH-EE-AH
AH-NEE-YELL
AZZ-ARE-EE-AH-WHO
REH-HAW

The Ritual of The Empowered Mind

This ritual connects you to the strength within your mind so that it becomes empowered, enabling you to impose your will over many situations.

Every act is an act of change, of transformation, and an expression of who we are in any given moment. Every emotion we experience is a response to our history as well as the events confronting us at that moment. Life itself, although seemingly chaotic and random, can be a series of offers that we choose to accept or reject, and in doing so, we shape the course of our lives.

With magick, it is possible to guide events more directly. With mystical power, it is possible to connect to your deepest mind, where it mingles with your soul. This empowers your subconscious and conscious minds, enabling you to have a better understanding of who you are and much greater power to apply your will to reality.

When your mind is empowered in this way, you are infused with a strength that is tangible, directly influencing the way others perceive and react to you. With an act of will, you can dismiss the plans and powers of an enemy. You can clear unwanted people, energies, and entities from any location.

When you are in a place of need, you will attract the help and love of those you need most, and when there is an ongoing problem, you will find the patience and strength to endure it without suffering.

The effort you make to progress in the world will be strengthened, and the help of others in all your endeavors will be increased. The speed at which you achieve your goals can increase. Others will see you as a leader, and you will experience a genuine sense of confidence in yourself because it comes from who you really are.

The light of the empowered mind can attract the unwanted, but you never shine this brightly without being given the will to remove those you do not want, and you will be protected from those who would wish to drain your energy.

If you have suffered from a weak will, being tempted, addicted, or locked into habits, the empowered mind gives you a strength unlike any you have experienced, to rise above such temptations with ease.

In cases where a situation appears to be locked, the empowered mind can give you clues about how to circumvent the obvious problems and find a cunning way to victory. You may find that you find ways to shed aspects of yourself that are holding you back from being all you want to be.

The empowered mind will enable you to see where your life can be most effectively changed by willpower, imagination, or magick. You will perceive the places in your life where there is motion, where reality is most likely to yield. By discovering these foundations, and directing your efforts at them, you achieve far more than when you tackle problems on the surface.

The Ritual Words of The Empowered Mind

El is pronounced as ELL.

El Shaddai is pronounced as ELL-SHAD-EYE.

Tzoiaht is pronounced as TS-AWE-EE-AHT.

Sabkasbeiah is pronounced as SAB-KASS-BEH-EE-AH.

Amediel is pronounced as AM-EH-DEE-YELL.

Iehodel is pronounced as EE-EH-AWE-DEH-ELL.

Eshal is pronounced as ESH-AHL.

The Empowered Mind Sigil

ELL
ELL-SHAD-EYE
TS-AWE-EE-AHT
SAB-KASS-BEH-EE-AH
AM-EH-DEE-YELL
EE-EH-AWE-DEH-ELL
ESH-AHL

Experiencing the Mystical

In reading about the seven main rituals in this part of the book, it is easy to focus on the possible results, even though I have maintained throughout that the results are only a possible side effect. This is because the mystical, by definition, cannot be explained. It can only be experienced.

I wrote about the results to give an impression of the power of those rituals. It gives you a clue as to the nature of these mystical powers. I could have told you to perform rituals for Perception, Knowledge, Love, Healing, Imagination, Transformation and The Empowered Mind, without giving any further details, and if you performed the rituals, all the effects could flow into your life without you ever knowing about them beforehand. I did not do that because I believe it would feel too abstract, without giving you any hope or motivation. A taste of the powers may encourage you to invite them within. You may receive intuitive guidance on how to do this, or find that you develop the ability to work with the powers effortlessly. If you merely observe nature, or perform a more formal practice such as meditation, you may find you are led to experience periods of pure ecstasy.

The focus of Part One is the spiritual experience and so I suggest that now you have read about the powers and the results they may bring, you perform the rituals as described, as works of the spirit and soul, without focusing on those powers. Equally, you do not need to reach or yearn for the mystical. But I will say that mystical experiences are as likely as anything else, even though they have barely been mentioned. What is meant by mystical is open to interpretation, but when you sense the compassion of the universe, the interconnectedness of things, and the meaning hidden in the ordinary, you will be catching sight of the mystical, and you will gain a greater understanding of who you are and all that you are meant to achieve.

Part Two: World Changing

The rituals in Part Two are for direct change. Although they are connected to the mystical undercurrents of Part One, they are used when you want a specific result.

As you look through them, you might wonder why the rituals are just presented in a long list, rather than ordered into rituals of love, rituals of perception, and so on. There is a very important and deliberate reason for this.

It's tempting to look at a ritual, and notice that it is probably connected to, for example, *The Ritual of Love*. You can see that some of the words are the same, and the power you want to use is similar to one that's described in *The Ritual of Love* chapter. Doesn't it make sense that you should also use *The Ritual of Love* at the same time? The answer may seem strange, but you should not seek out a specific ritual from Part One to help empower these rituals.

If you want to improve their power, you should use at least one of the seven main rituals from Part One, but you should not choose one to deliberately enhance the effect. This might seem like a minor point, but it's not. To make a choice like that goes against the essence of the method described in Part One.

If you happen to be using a Part One ritual that seems connected, or if you're using them all, that's fine, but there is a subtlety to this process. All I am asking you to do is separate the work you do in Part One from the work you do here in Part Two. Let the workings of Part One be what they are, and use these rituals in Part Two when you need them.

Using at least one of the rituals from Part One on a regular basis will help with these rituals, even if you only perform something once a week. Part One causes a softening of reality that makes all magick more capable of working, while protecting you from outside influence.

The rituals in Part Two only need to be performed once. What follows is a description of the ritual process used in this part of the book, and you will notice that it is different to Part One. If you have read either *Words of Power* or *The Greater Words of Power*, it will be somewhat familiar.

You should, of course, have used *The Attuning Ritual*, and you should have performed at least one ritual from Part One. You then choose a ritual that seems appropriate for your needs.

Contemplate the change

Sit in a quiet place, and gaze at the sigil with your focus on the white space and the outer black circles. See Part One (Step 4.) for full details of this technique. As you gaze, contemplate the problem, challenge or aspect of your life that you want to change. Notice how the problem makes you feel. At this point, you are not trying to find a solution or imagine how things could change. Feel the pain, discomfort, or other emotions that surround the issue. Your feelings do not have to be strong, but notice how you feel when you think about the subject of your magick.

If, for example, you want to use the ritual to *Experience Improved Intuition*, it is probably because you are frustrated by your lack of intuition. Even if the feeling isn't as strong as lack, and is only desire for more intuition than you have, that is a feeling you can work with. Whatever you feel is valid, so *feel* it, and spend about a minute experiencing this feeling. (There is no need to scan the outer letter-circle, or to perform the Associated Action from Part One.)

Scan the sigil

Scan each word in the sigil, looking at the letter shapes from right to left. This is the same as in Part One. Start with the uppermost word and work your way down the list.

During this visual scan you may feel the negative emotions from contemplating the desired change, and that is fine. If the emotion fades away, that is also fine. For this part of the process, keep your focus on scanning the words.

Experience the solution

Before speaking the words, imagine the relief and gratitude you would feel if your problem was solved. This transmutes your emotion from the negative emotion you felt earlier, to match the positive emotion you want to achieve.

If the magick worked, how would you feel? That's all you have to imagine. And imagine it *as though it's already happened*. You might feel elated, calm, joyous, or something else, but let yourself feel the emotion, as though you have the result right now. And feel grateful that you feel so good.

Do not concern yourself with how the result might be achieved. Do not try to think about the steps required for the problem to be solved. If you're looking to *Improve Your Ability to Vizualize*, you don't need to think about the steps you'll take. Not yet. You just imagine how good it would feel to master that skill. Your focus should be on the result you want, not how you get there.

The feeling does not have to be intense or clear. Just catch a hint of the feeling, and the transmutation will empower your magick. Once you have that feeling, speak the Words of Power.

Speak the words

Continue to feel the emotion, and now speak the Words of Power. They are printed beneath the sigil. These are read as though they are English, from left to right. Read each word, just once, and as you say the word, feel the emotion of your desired result. Then move to the next word on the next line. If the emotion fades slightly as you continue, that's fine, but try to maintain a feeling of gratitude, as though the magick has already worked.

Between each spoken word, glance up at the sigil for a moment, casually and without trying to see a specific word, and then speak the next word in the list. Refer to the notes on speaking the words in Part One to get this right.

Let go of the result

When you speak the final word, the magick is over, you should allow it to work. You do this by trusting it. If you don't actually trust it or believe in it, you can act *as though* you trust it by taking your attention off the magick. Assume you'll get what you asked for.

If you keep checking whether or not the magick has worked, or counting how many hours and days have passed since your ritual, you are lusting for result. This lust is the opposite of trust. Take your attention off the magick, and the magick will work better than when you pester it with anxious thoughts and impatience. If you find yourself thinking about the result you want, let yourself feel pleasure, as though the result has already come about. This helps you avoid lust for result.

You should also do your part to encourage the change to take place, taking any actions you can, especially if your intuition guides you to take new actions. If you do nothing and hope for the magick to take care of everything, it is far less likely to work. When you put in a small effort, the magick magnifies your effort more than you might imagine possible.

With some rituals, it's very clear how you can do your part, but with others it may seem like there is nothing you can do, and that is fine. In such cases, remain open to the magick working, and trust that the magick will develop in time.

Magickal results occur in ways that you might not expect, and when you least expect them. Always feel grateful for a result, even if it occurred with a slight twist. You do not need to call out to the Angels to thank them, but make sure that you enjoy the result, and feel grateful. The Angels will know.

Avoid writing off a result as a failure, just because it didn't manifest when you wanted it to. If you truly let go, and accept that the magick will work when the time is right, then the right time may come very soon. But if you say, 'That ritual didn't work,' through impatience, you stifle the magick. Leave your rituals open, and be grateful when the results come. Bear in mind that results can come to you instantly, or they can take three hours, three days, three weeks, three months, or more. Most of the time, people find this magick works exceptionally fast. If it does, accept the result with gratitude, but if it doesn't work as quickly as you want, know that patience will bring you the rewards you seek.

Resist the temptation to speak to the Angels directly during the ritual. I know some people have tried this, but it's not the best experiment. Speaking your desire in words will tend to confuse the message you're conveying to the Angels. They communicate using emotions, thought shapes and an understanding of aspects of your being that you don't even know how to put into words. They bring messages from within you. This all works very easily if you follow the instructions above. But if you speak to the Angels, or pray or ask for something, your words actually conjure up a host of conflicting doubts, fears, desires, and all sorts of emotions that muddy the message. Trust that the method works with your feelings alone and it will work.

The Rituals in Part One cannot be used directly to help another person, because they are not directed in any way. Some of the rituals in Part Two can be used to help other people. A ritual such as *Be Seen in a Chosen Way* is unlikely to help somebody else unless you know for certain how they want to be seen. In such cases it is wiser to introduce somebody to magick so they can learn the technique themselves.

For a ritual such as *Restore Health When an Illness has Passed*, you could easily use that to help a loved one, without them even knowing. When performing the ritual imagine that you are the other person, and imagine the emotional change they would feel if they performed the ritual. It's like pretending to be that person and feeling their relief. Even if you can't actually imagine being the other person, you should be able to imagine how they would feel at the outset and what their relief might feel during the transmutation.

You might want a list of which rituals work well for others, but I have learned that it is far wiser to let you work this out for yourself. Read about the ritual, and think about how it might work for another person, and if you can think of a way to use it for somebody else, feel free to do so. Always consider that it is difficult to know what other people really want, and that interfering may not be the best idea. But if you feel the need to help, you can. Overall, though, the greatest benefits are found by directing the magick to affect your reality, either by making changes in you or by influencing people that affect you.

On the following pages you will find a description of the ritual powers on the left-hand page. The sigil appears on the right-hand page, with the Words of Power listed below. It is quite safe to scan through the book and look at the sigils as you search for the magick you need. Nothing will happen by accident, and the magick only works when you intend for it to work.

You may find that the rituals in Part One bring everything you need, but should you require more directed magick, there are many rituals here that can be used creatively to change your world.

Be Seen by Those You Care About

When you care for friends or lovers, but they do not seem to notice you, it can be frustrating. Even within your own home or workplace, you can feel like you've disappeared. There are many reasons this happens, and they can be both internal and external, but whatever the cause, you can choose to be seen again by those you care about.

When performing the ritual, you can direct the energy at an individual, if you feel that one person no longer sees you for who you are. If you are feeling ignored by most people you care about, use that feeling to be seen by all those people.

Note that this ritual is designed to work on people you care about. It won't make you more visible to somebody you dislike, and won't attract attention generally. It works to make the people you care about see you, notice your needs, and be more willing to connect with you.

El is pronounced as ELL.
El Shaddai is pronounced as ELL-SHAD-EYE.
Iruraiah is pronounced as EE-ROO-RAH-EE-AH.
Yanevivael is pronounced as YAN-EV-EE-VAH-ELL.
Orpaniel is pronounced as OAR-PAH-NEE-ELL.
Reqahti is pronounced as RECK-AH-TEE.
Hayi is pronounced as HAH-YEE-EE.

ELL
ELL-SHAD-EYE
EE-ROO-RAH-EE-AH
YAN-EV-EE-VAH-ELL
OAR-PAH-NEE-ELL
RECK-AH-TEE
HAH-YEE-EE

Be Seen in a Chosen Way

You may want people to see you in a specific way, and this ritual can influence others to perceive you in that way. If you want to be seen as a leader rather than a follower, or courageous rather than a coward, you can choose to create that perception in others.

This works because people use mental shortcuts to summarize what they think, and these mental summaries, once formed, rarely change unless directly influenced. This ritual works on that aspect of the mind to bring about a change in perception. The challenge with this ritual is that when people perceive you to be a certain way they will expect you to act that way. If you influence people to perceive you as being highly social and begin a relationship with somebody based on that, it might be confusing and destructive if you don't act in a social way.

My advice, therefore, is to use this not to create an illusion, but to ensure that people see a true quality that you believe is within you, but one that people often miss. It is all too common to be a strong person who is seen as weak, or an intelligent person who is seen as stupid. With this ritual, you can change that so you are perceived fairly. In some cases, you may want to exaggerate a quality a little, but don't overdo it, for the reasons given above.

You might be wondering what to do if you change your mind after you've performed the ritual. All you need to do is perform it again, choosing an alternate way that you wish to be perceived.

El is pronounced as ELL.
El Shaddai is pronounced as ELL-SHAD-EYE.
Iruraiah is pronounced as EE-ROO-RAH-EE-AH.
Yanevivael is pronounced as YAN-EV-EE-VAH-ELL.
Orpaniel is pronounced as OAR-PAH-NEE-ELL.
Nerentaq is pronounced as NEH-RENT-ACK.
Hayi is pronounced as HAH-YEE-EE.

ELL
ELL-SHAD-EYE
EE-ROO-RAH-EE-AH
YAN-EV-EE-VAH-ELL
OAR-PAH-NEE-ELL
NEH-RENT-ACK
HAH-YEE-EE

Become More Noticeable to People

If you feel like you are not noticed by people in social situations, use this ritual to ensure that people acknowledge you. The ritual works in a way that makes you seem fascinating. People will want to include you in conversations. What you do with that, once the conversation begins, is up to you, but the magick works to make you stand out from the crowd and exude a warmth that makes people want to know you.

El is pronounced as ELL.
El Shaddai is pronounced as ELL-SHAD-EYE.
Iruraiah is pronounced as EE-ROO-RAH-EE-AH.
Yanevivael is pronounced as YAN-EV-EE-VAH-ELL.
Orpaniel is pronounced as OAR-PAH-NEE-ELL.
Avarneh is pronounced as AH-VAR-NEH.
Hayi is pronounced as HAH-YEE-EE.

ELL
ELL-SHAD-EYE
EE-ROO-RAH-EE-AH
YAN-EV-EE-VAH-ELL
OAR-PAH-NEE-ELL
AH-VAR-NEH
HAH-YEE-EE

Experience Improved Intuition

In almost every magick book and countless self-help books, authors frequently say you should trust your intuition. I say this all the time, and I know it can be frustrating for some people because they don't believe they have good intuition. It is true that if you don't use your intuition, then your connection to it fades, but I do not believe anybody has poor intuition.

This ritual enables you to experience improved intuition by reconnecting you to your inherent ability to be intuitive. This can able you to better judge people and situations, to get a feeling for what might be happening in the present moment, and even for what may be to come. Intuition is a power that can profoundly affect your ability to make good choices and smooths out many situations.

El is pronounced as ELL.
El Shaddai is pronounced as ELL-SHAD-EYE.
Iruraiah is pronounced as EE-ROO-RAH-EE-AH.
Yanevivael is pronounced as YAN-EV-EE-VAH-ELL.
Orpaniel is pronounced as OAR-PAH-NEE-ELL.
Astiel is pronounced as ASS-TEE-ELL.
Hayi is pronounced as HAH-YEE-EE.

ELL
ELL-SHAD-EYE
EE-ROO-RAH-EE-AH
YAN-EV-EE-VAH-ELL
OAR-PAH-NEE-ELL
ASS-TEE-ELL
HAH-YEE-EE

Find Clarity When Confused

If you are feeling confused about a specific issue or situation, or if your mind feels overwhelmed with bewilderment, this ritual can bring you the clarity you need. It won't make any decisions for you or enable you to know every fact, but it will clear away the fog in your mind so you can gather facts and make decisions.

Whatever the cause of the confusion, you will find you are able to think clearly shortly after performing the ritual. This can be used to get over one period of confusion, and it can be used in a more general way if you feel your mind is often more confused than it should be.

El is pronounced as ELL.
El Shaddai is pronounced as ELL-SHAD-EYE.
Iruraiah is pronounced as EE-ROO-RAH-EE-AH.
Yanevivael is pronounced as YAN-EV-EE-VAH-ELL.
Orpaniel is pronounced as OAR-PAH-NEE-ELL.
Gemati is pronounced as GEH-MAH-TEE.
Hayi is pronounced as HAH-YEE-EE.

ELL
ELL-SHAD-EYE
EE-ROO-RAH-EE-AH
YAN-EV-EE-VAH-ELL
OAR-PAH-NEE-ELL
GEH-MAH-TEE
HAH-YEE-EE

Influence with Emotions

This is a ritual of direct influence, where you use the intensity of your emotions to affect how another person thinks or feels. Whether or not you choose to use such magick is down to your own moral and ethical judgment, but you may find there are times when you feel it is right to influence somebody directly.

Imagine you are unfairly blamed for something at work, and the boss believes everybody else. You will have strong emotions of anger and injustice. You can use that emotional power to change the mind of your boss.

To perform the ritual, you need to become aware of the intense emotions the situation has created and how your target's beliefs are a problem. In this example, you would recall your anger at the injustice and you would also consider how frustrating it is that your boss doesn't believe you. Then, as the ritual progresses, you perform the emotional transmutation and imagine how good it would feel to be free of those emotions and what a relief it would be for your boss to believe you.

It's a lot less complicated than it sounds. I used an example of injustice because this is one of the best ways to employ this ritual. It can also be used in any situation where your emotions have been driven to a highly intense level, and where changing somebody's mind would bring the relief you seek.

El is pronounced as ELL.
El Shaddai is pronounced as ELL-SHAD-EYE.
Iruraiah is pronounced as EE-ROO-RAH-EE-AH.
Yanevivael is pronounced as YAN-EV-EE-VAH-ELL.
Orpaniel is pronounced as OAR-PAH-NEE-ELL.
Sevelah is pronounced as SEH-VEH-LAH.
Hayi is pronounced as HAH-YEE-EE.

ELL
ELL-SHAD-EYE
EE-ROO-RAH-EE-AH
YAN-EV-EE-VAH-ELL
OAR-PAH-NEE-ELL
SEH-VEH-LAH
HAH-YEE-EE

Appear Trustworthy

The ritual will make you appear as though you are a trustworthy person. It is a ritual that distorts the perception of others, and it can be useful when you face a legal problem, when you move to a new job or home, or if your social and business interactions rely on trust. What I like about this ritual is that the Angelic power is infused with strength, so you never appear as somebody who is trustworthy out of fear, but as somebody who will keep their word because of a deep sense of honor.

El is pronounced as ELL.
El Shaddai is pronounced as ELL-SHAD-EYE.
Iruraiah is pronounced as EE-ROO-RAH-EE-AH.
Yanevivael is pronounced as YAN-EV-EE-VAH-ELL.
Orpaniel is pronounced as OAR-PAH-NEE-ELL.
Digal is pronounced as DEE-GAHL.
Hayi is pronounced as HAH-YEE-EE.

ELL
ELL-SHAD-EYE
EE-ROO-RAH-EE-AH
YAN-EV-EE-VAH-ELL
OAR-PAH-NEE-ELL
DEE-GAHL
HAH-YEE-EE

Attract Through Inner Light

There are many rituals that can make people be attracted to you, but this one works by projecting what is beautiful within you. I trust that within you there is great warmth, love, and a capacity for joy. Even if these aspects of your being are somewhat dormant, the ritual can help them shine from within you, and thus make them more likely to become real in your life.

You only need to perform this ritual once, feeling frustration that your inner light, the depth of your being, is hidden from those who might be attracted to you. This changes to relief as the ritual progresses, and the result will often be immediately noticeable. The changes will strengthen over the coming days and weeks.

There is no guarantee that people will like you when they get to know you, but the odds are in your favor because the magick works not through illusion, but by revealing who you are and what is beautiful about you. Anybody who could potentially be attracted to you will be attracted to you.

El is pronounced as ELL.
El Shaddai is pronounced as ELL-SHAD-EYE.
Iruraiah is pronounced as EE-ROO-RAH-EE-AH.
Yanevivael is pronounced as YAN-EV-EE-VAH-ELL.
Orpaniel is pronounced as OAR-PAH-NEE-ELL.
Kiladah is pronounced as KEY-LAH-DAH.
Hayi is pronounced as HAH-YEE-EE.

ELL
ELL-SHAD-EYE
EE-ROO-RAH-EE-AH
YAN-EV-EE-VAH-ELL
OAR-PAH-NEE-ELL
KEY-LAH-DAH
HAH-YEE-EE

Attract a Following

A few decades ago, attracting a following meant gradually building a fanbase because of the quality of your creative work. At the time this book is being written people try to gain followers on social media in a few weeks. For people who work in the arts, there is enormous pressure to gain a large number of followers.

Using this ritual, when you put in the effort to be seen, whether online or in the real world, you will have a better chance of making people want to see more of who you are and what you do.

This is not only for social media. You might be an artist in a small city or a band that tours a certain part of the country. Gaining a following may have nothing to do with social media at all.

If you do nothing to attract a following, fans won't appear spontaneously. If you are trying to build a following, you will find that your efforts are perceived as more fascinating, bringing pleasure to the people who see or experience them. The magick doesn't directly influence people to follow you but makes them more likely to desire your work, and that should, in turn, enable them to become followers of your work. If you aim this at social media, the entire system is designed to obtain followers, but if you are not using social media, use something else. Give people a way to follow you, such as an exhibition space where you regularly appear or a venue where you perform every month.

The quality of results will ultimately depend on how good your work is, but I know of many people who produce good material and struggle to gain a following. If you are good at what you do, this ritual can help you garner the following you deserve.

El is pronounced as ELL.
El Shaddai is pronounced as ELL-SHAD-EYE.
Iruraiah is pronounced as EE-ROO-RAH-EE-AH.
Yanevivael is pronounced as YAN-EV-EE-VAH-ELL.
Orpaniel is pronounced as OAR-PAH-NEE-ELL.
Ateneni is pronounced as AH-TEN-EN-EE.
Hayi is pronounced as HAH-YEE-EE.

ELL
ELL-SHAD-EYE
EE-ROO-RAH-EE-AH
YAN-EV-EE-VAH-ELL
OAR-PAH-NEE-ELL
AH-TEN-EN-EE
HAH-YEE-EE

Find Hope in a Difficult Time

There are rituals in this book that can help you cope with overwhelm and disruption, but this ritual is designed for those times when you know that all you need is hope. During a difficult time, you may find that you lose all sense of hope, and that makes you less able to solve your problems and emerge from the crisis. The ritual can be used for any event you consider challenging, from taking exams to undergoing a difficult course of medical treatment. When you need hope, it will be restored.

El is pronounced as ELL.
El Shaddai is pronounced as ELL-SHAD-EYE.
Sehahsiah is pronounced as SEH-AH-SEE-AH.
Shameshiel is pronounced as SHAH-MEH-SHE-YELL.
Orpaniel is pronounced as OAR-PAH-NEE-ELL.
Aleven is pronounced as AH-LEV-EN.
Vesher is pronounced as VEH-SHAR.

ELL
ELL-SHAD-EYE
SEH-AH-SEE-AH
SHAH-MEH-SHE-YELL
OAR-PAH-NEE-ELL
AH-LEV-EN
VEH-SHAR

Catch a Glimpse of Possible Futures

This part of the book is based on problem-solving rituals, but the mystical pervades the magick, sometimes more noticeably than others. Here, you will sense the mystical more than usual. The ritual will not guide you directly by offering instructive divination, but when you gain an impression of the futures that may await you, your options become more evident.

In glimpsing several of your possible futures, both in the near and far future, you are better able to make decisions in the present. Knowing what may come can help you choose to seek that future, or in some cases, to avoid it completely.

When performing the ritual, consider the potential of the magick to benefit your life, because this helps you to generate the required feelings. When you contemplate the change you desire, feel discomfort at your inability to catch glimpses of your possible futures. This may sound abstract, but if you try it, you'll find that you can generate this feeling. You then feel relief and gratitude at developing this ability and the benefits it will bring.

Following the ritual, you can allow visions, images, and impressions to arise spontaneously as the days and weeks pass, or you can meditate on the future at any time you like. This is a curious power but one with a surprising amount of potential.

El is pronounced as ELL.
El Shaddai is pronounced as ELL-SHAD-EYE.
Sehahsiah is pronounced as SEH-AH-SEE-AH.
Shameshiel is pronounced as SHAH-MEH-SHE-YELL.
Orpaniel is pronounced as OAR-PAH-NEE-ELL.
Ivaven is pronounced as EE-VAH-VAH-EN.
Vesher is pronounced as VEH-SHAR.

ELL
ELL-SHAD-EYE
SEH-AH-SEE-AH
SHAH-MEH-SHE-YELL
OAR-PAH-NEE-ELL
EE-VAH-VAH-EN
VEH-SHAR

Develop Rational Optimism

Optimism is said to make you achieve more and live longer, but when that optimism is based on self-deception, there is a danger that it can lead to poor decision-making. In writing this chapter, I know that this power will not be widely sought, and sounds anything but mystical. I urge you to try this at some point, perhaps when there are no other pressing issues.

You may think that rational optimism is a feeling based purely on facts, but it's a little weirder than that. What I call rational optimism is the most positive feeling you can obtain when you sense the facts, the context of those facts, as well as truths you obtain through intuition.

When you begin the ritual, you only need to feel that you lack rational optimism, as described above. You then feel relief at obtaining this ability. The result is that you will become more optimistic, but not in a way that feels forced. Your optimism will be based on your full and intuitive understanding of the situations that arise in your life

El is pronounced as ELL.
El Shaddai is pronounced as ELL-SHAD-EYE.
Sehahsiah is pronounced as SEH-AH-SEE-AH.
Shameshiel is pronounced as SHAH-MEH-SHE-YELL.
Orpaniel is pronounced as OAR-PAH-NEE-ELL.
Teravavair is pronounced as TEH-RAH-VAH-VAIR.
Vesher is pronounced as VEH-SHAR.

ELL
ELL-SHAD-EYE
SEH-AH-SEE-AH
SHAH-MEH-SHE-YELL
OAR-PAH-NEE-ELL
TEH-RAH-VAH-VAIR
VEH-SHAR

Discover Your Authentic Potential

This ritual helps you to discover your authentic potential in relation to a specific activity. It doesn't give you an overview of your whole life but helps you see whether you'd be a good novelist, racing driver, teacher, lawyer, or anything else you might be dreaming of becoming.

You can use the ritual before you begin the pursuit of your dream or ambition, or when you have been pursuing it for some time. In the days and weeks that follow you should gain an impression of how you actually feel about your dream, and a strong sense of how much you could achieve if you pursue your goals.

For this to work effectively, you need to remain open to all feelings, visions, and sensations that occur to you, even if they aren't what you want to believe. Don't assume that the first feeling you obtain is the end of the story. After some time, you should have gained an intuitive understanding of your authentic potential regarding this dream.

Performing the ritual can be disheartening if you discover that your potential is more limited than you want. It can be equally alarming to find that you have discovered a true path to success. Remember that magick is about making decisions, not being chained by fate. Even if this ritual reveals less potential than you hoped for, you have the option to change your destiny by working on the areas that will improve your potential. Knowing your current potential is better than fooling yourself. You then have the option to take a different path or to work so hard on improving your abilities that when you perform this ritual again, you will see that your authentic potential has shifted.

El is pronounced as ELL.
El Shaddai is pronounced as ELL-SHAD-EYE.
Sehahsiah is pronounced as SEH-AH-SEE-AH.
Shameshiel is pronounced as SHAH-MEH-SHE-YELL.
Orpaniel is pronounced as OAR-PAH-NEE-ELL.
Kadiel is pronounced as KAH-DEE-YELL.
Vesher is pronounced as VEH-SHAR.

ELL
ELL-SHAD-EYE
SEH-AH-SEE-AH
SHAH-MEH-SHE-YELL
OAR-PAH-NEE-ELL
KAH-DEE-YELL
VEH-SHAR

Find Wisdom to Make a Decision

You make hundreds of minor decisions every day, and many quite major decisions each year. There are some decisions, however, that make you feel at a loss. It can feel as though you don't have the wisdom or foresight to guess how things will work out.

When you are faced with a decision like this, use this ritual to gain the required wisdom. It works by enabling you to see the facts objectively, as well as improving your understanding of your emotional needs, while giving you a mystical sense of how the various decisions might play out.

After you've performed the ritual, you should forget about the decision for a time, if there's sufficient time to do so, and then instead of thinking about the decision in an ordinary way, sit quietly and let the decision come into your mind. You will find that you gain a much more expansive feeling of what the decision means and how best to proceed.

If you have to make the decision rapidly, you can sit with the problem in your mind as soon as the ritual is over, but in an ideal case, you should allow some hours or days to pass, and you may find that moments of insight and inspiration occur to you unexpectedly.

El is pronounced as ELL.
El Shaddai is pronounced as ELL-SHAD-EYE.
Sehahsiah is pronounced as SEH-AH-SEE-AH.
Shameshiel is pronounced as SHAH-MEH-SHE-YELL.
Orpaniel is pronounced as OAR-PAH-NEE-ELL.
Kareteh is pronounced as KAH-REH-TEH.
Vesher is pronounced as VEH-SHAR.

ELL
ELL-SHAD-EYE
SEH-AH-SEE-AH
SHAH-MEH-SHE-YELL
OAR-PAH-NEE-ELL
KAH-REH-TEH
VEH-SHAR

Understand Financial Decisions

This ritual is useful for people who struggle with everyday financial decisions, as well as those who work in business or finance. The underlying power gives you the ability to perceive and understand matters of symbolic exchange. In other words, you understand decisions that involve money, and you sense how they will affect your life.

If you work in the financial sector or run a business, you will be faced with an ongoing flow of financial decisions. You should use the ritual to improve your overall ability to understand economic processes. This means that when the options are in front of you, you gain a rational understanding as well as an ability to sense how your decisions will manifest in the future.

If you're not a financial wizard there are still many times when you need to understand a financial decision. When you're being offered a loan, a mortgage, or any kind of financial deal, you may feel that you're in over your head. It's often a good idea to hire a reputable and independent professional to help with these decisions, but magick can help you to understand the options laid before you.

Before you actually make the decision, you will understand what it means, and you will sense the long-term impact of the decision. This ritual can be performed each time there is a major financial decision. It's like going to see your accountant; nobody wants to do it, even though it can save you many thousands of dollars. You work hard to make money, but then you can lose so much by making one bad decision. This ritual is one of the most effective forms of money magick because it gives you the wisdom to create, grow, and enjoy your money.

El is pronounced as ELL.
El Shaddai is pronounced as ELL-SHAD-EYE.
Sehahsiah is pronounced as SEH-AH-SEE-AH.
Shameshiel is pronounced as SHAH-MEH-SHE-YELL.
Orpaniel is pronounced as OAR-PAH-NEE-ELL.
Anif is pronounced as AH-NEEF.
Vesher is pronounced as VEH-SHAR.

ELL
ELL-SHAD-EYE
SEH-AH-SEE-AH
SHAH-MEH-SHE-YELL
OAR-PAH-NEE-ELL
AH-NEEF
VEH-SHAR

Know the True Intentions of Others

It's been established by scientists that even good, honest people lie many times each day, and most of this is harmless social lubrication to take away unnecessary friction within our daily interactions. Sometimes, though, you need to know what somebody truly intends because there is more at stake.

When somebody tells you that they want to go into business with you, or that they plan to marry you, or that moving to a new country would be a good idea, you need to know if it's true.

When big decisions like this are being planned, true intentions are often hidden. In some cases, people hide their intentions because they aren't sure of them, and in other cases, they hide them because they don't want you to know the truth. You can use this ritual when you want to know somebody's true intentions. It doesn't have to be used when you suspect something is being hidden, only when you feel a definite need to know the truth. The result may be that the other person tells you the truth, or it may be that you gain a strong sense of knowing, where you are able to perceive the truth of the matter in a more mystical way.

El is pronounced as ELL.
El Shaddai is pronounced as ELL-SHAD-EYE.
Sehahsiah is pronounced as SEH-AH-SEE-AH.
Shameshiel is pronounced as SHAH-MEH-SHE-YELL.
Orpaniel is pronounced as OAR-PAH-NEE-ELL.
Teket is pronounced as TEH-KET.
Vesher is pronounced as VEH-SHAR.

ELL
ELL-SHAD-EYE
SEH-AH-SEE-AH
SHAH-MEH-SHE-YELL
OAR-PAH-NEE-ELL
TEH-KET
VEH-SHAR

See Beyond Fear

Many circumstances can make you fearful. With phobias, where there is no real threat, the fear can be a minor problem. In some cases, as with a fear of flying, it can disrupt your life. Other times, fear is based on an accurate assessment of the situation you find yourself in, but the level of fear you experience may be damaging to your ability to cope. If you feel that any fear is too intense, and is affecting your ability to enjoy life, this ritual can help reduce the fear. You may sense the Angels giving you clarity and objectivity, with their compassion making you able to see beyond fear. The ability to see a future beyond the fear is especially useful in drawn-out situations where there is ongoing fear for weeks or months. In those situations, this ritual can enable you to see beyond the potential disaster and therefore make the experience easier.

El is pronounced as ELL.
El Shaddai is pronounced as ELL-SHAD-EYE.
Bazraziah is pronounced as BAZZ-RAH-ZEE-AH.
Leoriel is pronounced as LEH-AWE-REE-YELL.
Orpaniel is pronounced as OAR-PAH-NEE-ELL.
Apikah is pronounced as AH-PEA-KAH.
Lav is pronounced as LAHV.

ELL
ELL-SHAD-EYE
BAZZ-RAH-ZEE-AH
LEH-AWE-REE-YELL
OAR-PAH-NEE-ELL
AH-PEA-KAH
LAHV

Stop Negative Thoughts

I am not a believer in positive thinking, because acceptance and experience of our emotions enables the useful ones to teach us, and the difficult ones to pass. Later in the book there is a ritual that deals with worry, when thoughts cycle in a negative way. This ritual is different, because it is directed at habits of negativity rather than cycles of worry.

There are sometimes situations where you have habitually negative thoughts about a person or experience that don't agree with what you really feel. In some relationships, for example, you may find that you have negative thoughts about a partner that cause you to bicker, or you may complain about a job that you actually like. In such cases, the habit of negativity is often a barrier to a more deeply hidden feeling. Rather than trying to work out what's going on in your psyche, this magickal shortcut stops the negative thoughts. You can aim the ritual at one area of your life, or if you find there is too much misplaced negativity throughout your life, use it to stop all such misplaced thoughts. Often, the ritual works by giving you a moment of perspective, so you can adjust your thoughts and allow them to be more authentic.

El is pronounced as ELL.
El Shaddai is pronounced as ELL-SHAD-EYE.
Bazraziah is pronounced as BAZZ-RAH-ZEE-AH.
Leoriel is pronounced as LEH-AWE-REE-YELL.
Orpaniel is pronounced as OAR-PAH-NEE-ELL.
Ralekah is pronounced as RAH-LEK-AH.
Lav is pronounced as LAHV.

ELL
ELL-SHAD-EYE
BAZZ-RAH-ZEE-AH
LEH-AWE-REE-YELL
OAR-PAH-NEE-ELL
RAH-LEK-AH
LAHV

Improve Imagination When Creating

The next ritual after this one is about visual imagination, but this ritual is about the ability to generate high-quality ideas when you are being creative. You might be creating music, writing a novel, or working in a creative industry. Any improvement in your ability to imagine will help. The form of imagination I am talking about here is the ability to make unexpected connections, to see ideas in a new way, or to discover something new that will improve the creation you are working on. If you work in the arts, or even if you have a hobby that requires this kind of imagination, you will benefit from the power of this ritual. If you need new ideas for projects, there is a ritual for that later in the book, but this ritual will give you an overall improvement in your ability to work imaginatively on all your creative projects.

El is pronounced as ELL.
El Shaddai is pronounced as ELL-SHAD-EYE.
Bazraziah is pronounced as BAZZ-RAH-ZEE-AH.
Leoriel is pronounced as LEH-AWE-REE-YELL.
Orpaniel is pronounced as OAR-PAH-NEE-ELL.
Ivatnah is pronounced as EE-VAH-TEH-NAH.
Lav is pronounced as LAHV.

ELL
ELL-SHAD-EYE
BAZZ-RAH-ZEE-AH
LEH-AWE-REE-YELL
OAR-PAH-NEE-ELL
EE-VAH-TEH-NAH
LAHV

Improve Your Ability to Visualize

In magick, the ability to visualize powerfully was once seen as the most important skill. In the seventies and eighties, there were whole branches of magick that were based on picturing your desires. It's now widely accepted that visual imagination is not as important as once thought, but nevertheless, the ability to imagine clearly has many practical applications in the ordinary world. It can be enjoyable for its own sake, but can also help in problem-solving. For creative people the benefits of improved visualization are extensive.

Following the ritual, you don't need to perform visualization exercises, but you should make an effort to use your visual imagination at any time where it might be appropriate. Where you might usually not bother to imagine something, because you believe your imagination to be weak, choose to picture what you can. This gives the magick an opportunity to work. You may also find your dreams become more vivid in the first few weeks. You only need to repeat this ritual if, after a noticeable improvement, you want to take the intensity of your imagination up another notch.

El is pronounced as ELL.
El Shaddai is pronounced as ELL-SHAD-EYE.
Bazraziah is pronounced as BAZZ-RAH-ZEE-AH.
Leoriel is pronounced as LEH-AWE-REE-YELL.
Orpaniel is pronounced as OAR-PAH-NEE-ELL.
Lelahf is pronounced as LEH-LAHF.
Lav is pronounced as LAHV.

ELL
ELL-SHAD-EYE
BAZZ-RAH-ZEE-AH
LEH-AWE-REE-YELL
OAR-PAH-NEE-ELL
LEH-LAHF
LAHV

Achieve with Less Effort

Unless you are extremely wise, it's most likely that you are working too hard to achieve the results you obtain in life. The struggle to succeed, or even just to keep up with the competition, at work or in business, can easily lead to burnout. Many people feel that they are overworked and under-rewarded, with little time to spare away from work.

Using this ritual will enable you to see where your efforts are making an impact, and where time is being wasted. This alone will help you to achieve more with less effort by adjusting your work practice. The ritual also brings a sense of peace and ease to your work so that you are not struggling to achieve, but getting more done in a shorter time. It can work by improving concentration and energy levels, but also works in a more mystical way, as though manipulating time to enable you to achieve what you want in a shorter time. You can use the ritual for a specific project, or to achieve more with less effort in a more general way.

El is pronounced as ELL.
El Shaddai is pronounced as ELL-SHAD-EYE.
Bazraziah is pronounced as BAZZ-RAH-ZEE-AH.
Leoriel is pronounced as LEH-AWE-REE-YELL.
Orpaniel is pronounced as OAR-PAH-NEE-ELL.
Terakoiah is pronounced as TEH-RACK-AWE-EE-AH.
Lav is pronounced as LAHV.

ELL
ELL-SHAD-EYE
BAZZ-RAH-ZEE-AH
LEH-AWE-REE-YELL
OAR-PAH-NEE-ELL
TEH-RACK-AWE-EE-AH
LAHV

Find Ideas for New Projects

This is an inspiration ritual, but it is not for being generally more inspired. You use this each time there is a new project that requires original ideas. You may only use this once when you need ideas about changing your career. If you work in a creative industry, this might be a ritual you work with on many occasions, each time a new project comes around, and you want to tap into inspiration. Creative people find a way to become inspired when needed, rather than when the muse strikes. By calling the Angels, you call for inspiration, and so long as you don't try to rush or force results, you will be inspired.

El is pronounced as ELL.
El Shaddai is pronounced as ELL-SHAD-EYE.
Bazraziah is pronounced as BAZZ-RAH-ZEE-AH.
Leoriel is pronounced as LEH-AWE-REE-YELL.
Orpaniel is pronounced as OAR-PAH-NEE-ELL.
Perian is pronounced as PEH-REE-AHN.
Lav is pronounced as LAHV.

ELL
ELL-SHAD-EYE
BAZZ-RAH-ZEE-AH
LEH-AWE-REE-YELL
OAR-PAH-NEE-ELL
PEH-REE-AHN
LAHV

Convey Love to One in Need

When a friend or loved one is in need, it can be difficult to convey your love, whether they are on the other side of the world or in the same room. At times of distress, when there is bad news or some other form of suffering, you may feel at a loss because you are unable to offer loving support. This ritual is a way of sending your love to the other person so that they will feel loved and supported and may regain some hope and perspective. It won't cure the problem but can make them feel love during a time of need.

During the ritual you only need to focus on the distress you feel at being unable to convey loving support, and then feel relief that the other person will now be supported by the sensation of your love. Sometimes, you will never hear a word about the experience from the other person, but there are times when they will make contact at a later date and tell you they felt your loving presence.

El is pronounced as ELL.
El Shaddai is pronounced as ELL-SHAD-EYE.
Satsatekiah is pronounced as SAH-TSAH-TEH-KEE-AH.
Ladediel is pronounced as LAH-DEH-DEE-YELL.
Orpaniel is pronounced as OAR-PAH-NEE-ELL.
Avebah is pronounced as AH-VEH-BAH.
Yelah is pronounced as YEH-LAH.

ELL
ELL-SHAD-EYE
SAH-TSAH-TEH-KEE-AH
LAH-DEH-DEE-YELL
OAR-PAH-NEE-ELL
AH-VEH-BAH
YEH-LAH

Find Relief from Melancholy

Melancholy is a feeling of sadness or unease that has no apparent cause. It can be a precursor to or element of depression, and if you suspect that this is the case, you should seek professional help. For those times when your emotional state is low, and you cannot see a reason, this ritual can help you to emerge from the darkness of those feelings. Although you shouldn't expect immediate results, this is a ritual where many people describe feeling Angelic sustenance immediately. If that isn't the case, then allow whatever time is required, and you should find the melancholy eases. Rituals don't need repeating unless something changes, so a single episode of melancholy can be addressed with a single ritual. If the melancholy returns sooner rather than later it may indicate an underlying cause that needs professional investigation.

El is pronounced as ELL.
El Shaddai is pronounced as ELL-SHAD-EYE.
Satsatekiah is pronounced as SAH-TSAH-TEH-KEE-AH.
Ladediel is pronounced as LAH-DEH-DEE-YELL.
Orpaniel is pronounced as OAR-PAH-NEE-ELL.
Netenal is pronounced as NEH-TEN-AHL.
Yelah is pronounced as YEH-LAH.

ELL
ELL-SHAD-EYE
SAH-TSAH-TEH-KEE-AH
LAH-DEH-DEE-YELL
OAR-PAH-NEE-ELL
NEH-TEN-AHL
YEH-LAH

Bring Forgiveness

In another part of the book, there is a ritual for forgiveness in the face of betrayal, but this ritual is less specific. It can help you to forgive a person or group of people when you wish to get past your bitterness. It can also be used to influence a group or an individual to forgive you for something you have done. If your feelings of regret or blame are strong, it can be difficult to undergo the emotional transmutation where you shift your feelings to relief and gratitude. As such, don't try too hard to generate the feelings at the start of the ritual because you only need a hint of emotion for this to work.

El is pronounced as ELL.
El Shaddai is pronounced as ELL-SHAD-EYE.
Satsatekiah is pronounced as SAH-TSAH-TEH-KEE-AH.
Ladediel is pronounced as LAH-DEH-DEE-YELL.
Orpaniel is pronounced as OAR-PAH-NEE-ELL.
Anevek is pronounced as AH-NEV-ECK.
Yelah is pronounced as YEH-LAH.

ELL
ELL-SHAD-EYE
SAH-TSAH-TEH-KEE-AH
LAH-DEH-DEE-YELL
OAR-PAH-NEE-ELL
AH-NEV-ECK
YEH-LAH

Uncover Honest Feelings

When you aren't even lying to yourself, that is when you have honest feelings. The structures of society and the habits of self-protection lead to feelings that may be far from the deepest we could have. The ritual could just as easily have been titled *Uncover Buried Feelings*, or *Understand What You Really Feel*. I call them honest feelings because when this ritual works, there is a strong feeling of honesty associated with the resultant emotions. It can be a risk to uncover your feelings, but it can help you to discover a more authentic life quite rapidly.

There are two ways to use this ritual. The first way is to direct it at yourself. Feel the frustration at being unsure about what you feel and then imagine the relief of knowing your honest feelings.

The second way to use this is when you want to know the honest feelings of somebody else. In most cases, this will be your partner or a potential partner. You feel frustration at being unsure of their feelings, and then feel relief at discovering them. Be aware that when used in this way it is a ritual of influence. It causes the other person to become aware of their honest feelings, and in turn, to communicate those feelings to you. What you find may not always be to your liking. This ritual could end a relationship in some cases. Use it only when you are certain that the truth is more important than illusion and comfort.

The results may become apparent within moments, or it may take some weeks for the realizations to occur. When aimed at another person, they may not be able to share what they feel until it's fully understood, but sometimes they will begin spilling out the revelations as they occur. This is potentially a beautiful and stabilizing ritual, but it can also cause great disruption, so be prepared.

El is pronounced as ELL.
El Shaddai is pronounced as ELL-SHAD-EYE.
Satsatekiah is pronounced as SAH-TSAH-TEH-KEE-AH.
Ladediel is pronounced as LAH-DEH-DEE-YELL.
Orpaniel is pronounced as OAR-PAH-NEE-ELL.
Keravi is pronounced as KEH-RAH-VEE.
Yelah is pronounced as YEH-LAH.

ELL
ELL-SHAD-EYE
SAH-TSAH-TEH-KEE-AH
LAH-DEH-DEE-YELL
OAR-PAH-NEE-ELL
KEH-RAH-VEE
YEH-LAH

Experience Underlying Passion

When your relationship has been based on passion in the past, but the dynamic is now calmer, this ritual can help to revive the physical and emotional desires required to renew the appetite for one another. It is not meant to stir feelings in somebody you have now broken up with, but is used in a current relationship to help make both partners reach the height of their physical attraction and lust.

As I've said elsewhere, Angels are beings of might and wonder, and they are capable of wielding powers that can stun people, and it is well within their abilities to arouse physical lust. It is not seen as unspiritual, but as an expression of the body, which is mingled with the soul, the heart, and the mind. The only limit on this ritual is that although it has the potential to stir whatever passion remains, in some cases the passion has gone forever. If the relationship has hardened into bitterness and bickering, the passion may have died.

In some cases, though, a relationship filled with bitterness and bickering can be saved by a reminder of the passion that underlies such tensions. If you feel tempted to use this ritual on a relationship, it is worth performing for understanding the relationship as well as for the pure pleasure that can result. It does not need to be repeated unless time restores a situation where the passion has once again dwindled.

El is pronounced as ELL.
El Shaddai is pronounced as ELL-SHAD-EYE.
Satsatekiah is pronounced as SAH-TSAH-TEH-KEE-AH.
Ladediel is pronounced as LAH-DEH-DEE-YELL.
Orpaniel is pronounced as OAR-PAH-NEE-ELL.
Girashevem is pronounced as GEE-RAH-SHEH-VEM.
Yelah is pronounced as YEH-LAH.

ELL
ELL-SHAD-EYE
SAH-TSAH-TEH-KEE-AH
LAH-DEH-DEE-YELL
OAR-PAH-NEE-ELL
GEE-RAH-SHEH-VEM
YEH-LAH

Open the Emotions Within Attraction

When you are attracted to somebody, and when you believe they are attracted to you, this ritual will allow emotions to manifest from the attraction more readily.

If there is no attraction, nothing will happen. If there is attraction, then your emotions and the emotions of the other person will begin to develop quite rapidly. This does not guarantee that everything will work out. Sometimes, the attraction is all there is, and the emotions in the other person don't develop enough to sustain a relationship. This can potentially be painful, because you may find that your emotions have increased greatly. So as in all matters of the heart you are taking a risk. Make sure you are willing to take that risk, and never assume that just because your love has grown, the other person will love you as much. Hopefully, they will, but it isn't guaranteed.

The other risk is that they may feel far more for you than you feel for them. Given these risks, is it ever wise to use this ritual? The ritual isn't designed for the impatient who are hoping to build the emotions more rapidly than would otherwise happen. Use it when you believe there is mutual attraction, and when some other factor is slowing the emotional growth. It could be that emotions are being ignored, repressed, or denied. If you are in that sort of situation, then you may find that this is an ideal ritual, because it means that the spark of attraction doesn't fade, opportunity isn't wasted, and that the potential for love is experienced. Be cautious, but don't be afraid, because mutual attraction is lovely, and when it converts into passion or love, that is a wonderful result.

El is pronounced as ELL.
El Shaddai is pronounced as ELL-SHAD-EYE.
Satsatekiah is pronounced as SAH-TSAH-TEH-KEE-AH.
Ladediel is pronounced as LAH-DEH-DEE-YELL.
Orpaniel is pronounced as OAR-PAH-NEE-ELL.
Echasepet is pronounced as EE-CHAH-SEH-PET.
Yelah is pronounced as YEH-LAH.

ELL
ELL-SHAD-EYE
SAH-TSAH-TEH-KEE-AH
LAH-DEH-DEE-YELL
OAR-PAH-NEE-ELL
EE-CHAH-SEH-PET
YEH-LAH

Heal a Relationship Damaged by Betrayal

Betrayal can occur in personal relationships, whether they are based on romance or friendship, and in all manner of other relationships such as business partnerships. You may be the one that has been betrayed, or you may have betrayed another. At an appropriate time, you may want to bring healing to the relationship.

Often, in the aftermath of betrayal, there is so much damage that everybody wants to move on and leave the past behind. That can be a sensible way to achieve healing. If, however, you find that there is too much to lose, and wish to forgive or be forgiven, this ritual can encourage healing in yourself and the other person.

Recovering from betrayal is rarely easy, and you often take a backward step every now and then, because the trust is difficult to rebuild. This ritual will help with trust, as well as calming other emotions, and opening hearts, so that forgiveness and acceptance are more likely.

El is pronounced as ELL.
El Shaddai is pronounced as ELL-SHAD-EYE.
Satsatekiah is pronounced as SAH-TSAH-TEH-KEE-AH.
Ladediel is pronounced as LAH-DEH-DEE-YELL.
Orpaniel is pronounced as OAR-PAH-NEE-ELL.
Rekahgal is pronounced as RECK-AH-GAHL.
Yelah is pronounced as YEH-LAH.

ELL
ELL-SHAD-EYE
SAH-TSAH-TEH-KEE-AH
LAH-DEH-DEE-YELL
OAR-PAH-NEE-ELL
RECK-AH-GAHL
YEH-LAH

Improve Friendship

A good friendship will usually develop without the need for magick. In some friendships, you may feel that there is potential for closer and warmer relations, but for reasons that aren't clear, that affection remains elusive. When you want the friendship to become more enjoyable, open, trusting, or to develop into a friendship you can rely on, use this ritual. This isn't a power that is widely sought, but on the rare occasions where you find a need for it, the results can be quite beautiful. It will not attract friends out of nowhere, and it does not work to generate romantic feelings in a friend, but when used as described, you will usually detect a change in the friendship quite rapidly.

El is pronounced as ELL.
El Shaddai is pronounced as ELL-SHAD-EYE.
Satsatekiah is pronounced as SAH-TSAH-TEH-KEE-AH.
Ladediel is pronounced as LAH-DEH-DEE-YELL.
Orpaniel is pronounced as OAR-PAH-NEE-ELL.
Chelien is pronounced as CHEH-LEE-EN.
Yelah is pronounced as YEH-LAH.

ELL
ELL-SHAD-EYE
SAH-TSAH-TEH-KEE-AH
LAH-DEH-DEE-YELL
OAR-PAH-NEE-ELL
CHEH-LEE-EN
YEH-LAH

Protect with Love

You can protect your loved ones, shielding them with the power of your love. As with all protection, it is not a shield from all life and every incident, but it does make a difference. Why use your love, and not the love of God, Angels or some other higher being? This magick uses Angelic power, but it is the quality of your love that makes it effective.

To perform the ritual, begin by considering how you feel when the person is not protected by your love. This might be a mild feeling but will still work when you transmute it during the ritual, to the feeling of relief that they are protected by your love.

There are many stories about people avoiding accidents when using protection magick. I often hear about people surviving car accidents in the days or hours after they perform a protection magick ritual. A cynical response to this is to say that if the protection were real, there would never have been a car crash. Others even say magick caused the car crash because magick is evil. I am sure you are already at the point where you can rise above such superstitious fear. Protection can sometimes make you avoid incidents and accidents completely but often works by shifting the odds slightly, so that you avoid disaster or injury. People have car crashes all the time, sadly, but for those with magick on their side, there can be a level of protection that feels miraculous. If you want to offer that sort of protection to somebody you love, in all areas of life, you can do so with this ritual.

El is pronounced as ELL.
El Shaddai is pronounced as ELL-SHAD-EYE.
Satsatekiah is pronounced as SAH-TSAH-TEH-KEE-AH.
Ladediel is pronounced as LAH-DEH-DEE-YELL.
Orpaniel is pronounced as OAR-PAH-NEE-ELL.
Secharori is pronounced as SECH-AH-RAW-REE.
Yelah is pronounced as YEH-LAH.

ELL
ELL-SHAD-EYE
SAH-TSAH-TEH-KEE-AH
LAH-DEH-DEE-YELL
OAR-PAH-NEE-ELL
SECH-AH-RAW-REE
YEH-LAH

Find Relief from Anxiety

Anybody with an anxiety disorder needs professional help, but if you find that anxiety is a problem, you can support your emotions and thought processes with magick. The ritual can be directed at general anxiety where you feel prone to being anxious all the time, or at anxiety that is triggered by many situations, or where a specific situation has arisen that is making you temporarily anxious.

As with all rituals, you contemplate the problem before imagining relief, but here you don't create anxiety itself for the sake of the ritual. Instead, acknowledge that having anxiety in your life is not a good feeling, and then go on to feel relief. This works without you having to generate anxious feelings, which would clearly be counter-productive. If you feel like the ritual might trigger anxiety, wait until you are in a more relaxed mood, so you can perform the ritual with confidence.

If you have already entered an anxious state and wish to relieve the anxiety immediately, all you need to do in the first part of the ritual is notice how you are feeling. Try not to fight it, but allow the feelings, and then try to imagine the relief you would feel if the anxiety went away. You may sense the strength, warmth, and compassion of the Angels.

If you use the ritual as just described, for temporary relief on one occasion, you should then consider using it more generally. That way, you can perform it just once more, and let it continue to work, rather than using it to tackle each anxious moment that occurs.

El is pronounced as ELL.
El Shaddai is pronounced as ELL-SHAD-EYE.
Qelileqaliah is pronounced as KELL-EE-LEK-AH-LEE-AH.
Michael is pronounced as MEEK-AH-ELL.
Orpaniel is pronounced as OAR-PAH-NEE-ELL.
Alenav is pronounced as AH-LEH-NAHV.
Mahash is pronounced as MAH-HAHSH.

ELL
ELL-SHAD-EYE
KELL-EE-LEK-AH-LEE-AH
MEEK-AH-ELL
OAR-PAH-NEE-ELL
AH-LEH-NAHV
MAH-HAHSH

Break the Cycle of Worry

It's easy to think that worry is the same as anxiety, and often they are linked, with anxious people suffering from continual worry. The Angelic powers in this ritual are directed at breaking cycles of worry, regardless of whether you also suffer from anxiety. It is possible to worry without becoming anxious. Continual worry is incapacitating, extremely draining, and far less useful than thinking through a problem and then releasing it.

The potential of this ritual is to provide you with the peace, objectivity, and calm to look at your worries, briefly, and then let them go. This prevents the worry from bothering you persistently. It may take some time to get used to this, and it does rely on you choosing to spend some time each day deliberately looking over your worries and then allowing them to release. If you try this, the Angelic powers will support your efforts, and the cycles of worry can be broken.

Worrying is not a problem in itself, and is considered to be a useful way of problem-solving, so I am only talking about breaking the habitual, never-ending cycles of worry, where you repeat the same thoughts and fears over and over. By taking time to ponder your concerns and release them, you still have the ability to problem solve creatively, without the anguish of worry spoiling your pleasure.

El is pronounced as ELL.
El Shaddai is pronounced as ELL-SHAD-EYE.
Qelileqaliah is pronounced as KELL-EE-LEK-AH-LEE-AH.
Michael is pronounced as MEEK-AH-ELL.
Orpaniel is pronounced as OAR-PAH-NEE-ELL.
Tireli is pronounced as TEE-REH-LEE.
Mahash is pronounced as MAH-HAHSH.

ELL
ELL-SHAD-EYE
KELL-EE-LEK-AH-LEE-AH
MEEK-AH-ELL
OAR-PAH-NEE-ELL
TEE-REH-LEE
MAH-HAHSH

Find Peace When Overwhelmed

Despite our best efforts, good planning and excellent magick, everybody can find they are overwhelmed by current circumstances. This can happen when you take on too much work, when somebody dies, or when a whole series of conflicts and dramas occur at once.

If you are already in a state of distress due to emotional or psychological issues, or through pressure from within relationships, overwhelm can occur even when the circumstances don't appear overwhelming to other people. It is your experience that counts. If you feel that you are overwhelmed, or if you sense that overwhelm is imminent, use this ritual.

You don't need to consider every factor that is bothering you, only to feel the sense of being overwhelmed, and the relief you would gain from finding peace. The ritual will not deal with all the problems causing the overwhelm but will bring you peace during this time. This makes it easier to deal with all the situations, using magick or ordinary solutions. The peace it facilitates can give you clarity and strength, and often you will sense a compassionate presence protecting you through the difficult times.

El is pronounced as ELL.
El Shaddai is pronounced as ELL-SHAD-EYE.
Qelileqaliah is pronounced as KELL-EE-LEK-AH-LEE-AH.
Michael is pronounced as MEEK-AH-ELL.
Orpaniel is pronounced as OAR-PAH-NEE-ELL.
Alephi is pronounced as AH-LEFF-EE.
Mahash is pronounced as MAH-HAHSH.

ELL
ELL-SHAD-EYE
KELL-EE-LEK-AH-LEE-AH
MEEK-AH-ELL
OAR-PAH-NEE-ELL
AH-LEFF-EE
MAH-HAHSH

Maintain Good Health

Some people work on maintaining good health every day, making the best choices about diet, exercise, and obtaining regular medical checkups. If you are somebody who uses magick, it might be wise to add in a ritual that helps maintain good health. It would be ludicrous to suggest that this is going to fend off every illness, but it can work to help you make the best choices and to provide an aura that can prevent your health from deteriorating.

When performing a ritual, you usually contemplate a problem you wish to change. With this ritual, you do not have a problem, so it requires a slightly different approach. Instead, you should imagine how bad it would feel if your good health was *not* maintained, and then as the ritual progresses you imagine (or remember) how good it feels to be healthy, and what a relief it is to have ongoing health. This is a slight twist in the technique, but it works.

The main challenge is choosing to perform the ritual. We all know that prevention is better than cure, but it's easier to deal with an issue once it becomes an obvious problem. If you are ever in a state of good health, I urge you to perform this ritual to give you the best chance of maintaining that condition. If you become ill at a future date, in a major or minor way, repeat this ritual when you are well again, to put the protection in place once more.

El is pronounced as ELL.
El Shaddai is pronounced as ELL-SHAD-EYE.
Qelileqaliah is pronounced as KELL-EE-LEK-AH-LEE-AH.
Michael is pronounced as MEEK-AH-ELL.
Orpaniel is pronounced as OAR-PAH-NEE-ELL.
Ashbah is pronounced as ASH-BAH.
Mahash is pronounced as MAH-HAHSH.

ELL
ELL-SHAD-EYE
KELL-EE-LEK-AH-LEE-AH
MEEK-AH-ELL
OAR-PAH-NEE-ELL
ASH-BAH
MAH-HAHSH

Prevent an Illness from Developing

Should you become unwell, a fast response is always wise to prevent the illness from developing. This is true in ordinary medical terms, where early intervention is far wiser than waiting until a condition is unbearable. It is also true with magick. Performing this ritual as soon as you become aware of sickness gives you the best chance of halting its development.

Due to the nature of health magick, and the number of charlatans making false promises, I would rather underplay these powers than tell you how effective they can be. I do not like false promises and do not want you to rely on magick at the expense of conventional medicine because to do so is dangerous. If you use these healing rituals, however, I hope you will find what many others have found, and that is a palpable energy that works to improve your condition.

Sometimes you feel healing energy during the ritual. At other times you may find that an illness develops no further, and you return to full health in a short time. In cases where the illness does take hold, your eventual recovery may be much faster than expected. All of this depends on the nature of the illness itself, so expect the magick to work, but accept whatever level of protection it provides.

El is pronounced as ELL.
El Shaddai is pronounced as ELL-SHAD-EYE.
Qelileqaliah is pronounced as KELL-EE-LEK-AH-LEE-AH.
Michael is pronounced as MEEK-AH-ELL.
Orpaniel is pronounced as OAR-PAH-NEE-ELL.
Siqmah is pronounced as SEE-KEM-AH.
Mahash is pronounced as MAH-HAHSH.

ELL
ELL-SHAD-EYE
KELL-EE-LEK-AH-LEE-AH
MEEK-AH-ELL
OAR-PAH-NEE-ELL
SEE-KEM-AH
MAH-HAHSH

Recover When Treatment is Underway

Throughout the book, I have recommended seeking conventional treatment for medical conditions, not only because it is logical, but because magick works best when it can support other forms of healing. If you are being treated by a professional, the energy of this ritual will give that treatment every possibility to work. This is true whether you are given a simple prescription or when surgery is required. Whatever the level of treatment, use this ritual as soon as you know that your sickness is going to be treated. That may mean performing the ritual as soon as you've seen a doctor, even if it's months before a planned surgery. If you've already started treatment, perform this ritual as soon as possible. It only needs to be performed once for any given condition, even if the treatment is ongoing.

El is pronounced as ELL.
El Shaddai is pronounced as ELL-SHAD-EYE.
Qelileqaliah is pronounced as KELL-EE-LEK-AH-LEE-AH.
Michael is pronounced as MEEK-AH-ELL.
Orpaniel is pronounced as OAR-PAH-NEE-ELL.
Abiel is pronounced as AH-BEE-ELL.
Mahash is pronounced as MAH-HAHSH.

ELL
ELL-SHAD-EYE
KELL-EE-LEK-AH-LEE-AH
MEEK-AH-ELL
OAR-PAH-NEE-ELL
AH-BEE-ELL
MAH-HAHSH

Restore Health When an Illness has Passed

Following any form of sickness, whether a major condition, a broken limb, or something as minor as the common cold, finding your way back to complete health can take time. This ritual should be used when you know the illness is over, or that the worst of it is over, and you wish to be restored to the full level of fitness and vitality you had before.

As with all rituals, you begin by contemplating pain or discomfort, and in this case, you are not contemplating a major discomfort, and that is fine. You only need to be aware of the fact that although the illness has passed, or almost passed, you are not fully restored. Feel this, and then as the ritual progresses, feel the relief of being restored to full health.

You may feel improvement immediately, but it may take time to feel as well as you did before the illness occurred. When you believe that your health has been fully restored, you may wish to perform the ritual to *Maintain Good Health*.

El is pronounced as ELL.
El Shaddai is pronounced as ELL-SHAD-EYE.
Qelileqaliah is pronounced as KELL-EE-LEK-AH-LEE-AH.
Michael is pronounced as MEEK-AH-ELL.
Orpaniel is pronounced as OAR-PAH-NEE-ELL.
Gavepar is pronounced as GAH-VEH-PAR.
Mahash is pronounced as MAH-HAHSH.

ELL
ELL-SHAD-EYE
KELL-EE-LEK-AH-LEE-AH
MEEK-AH-ELL
OAR-PAH-NEE-ELL
GAH-VEH-PAR
MAH-HAHSH

Find New Depths of Energy

There are two ways to use this ritual. The most effective way is when you are already vigorous and energetic, but wish to find more energy. If you are working on a large project or participating in sport, you may be doing well and feeling sustained, but you may still want more energy. I am not encouraging you to work so hard that you burn out, but you may sense that somewhere within there is a deeper well of energy. When you access that, you will be able to get more done, or achieve the same amount without feeling so tired at the end of each day.

The second way to use the ritual is when you are lacking energy, and need to find more. This is not always as effective because being drained can mean several factors are causing you to be exhausted, and all of them may need addressing, through magick or through ordinary efforts and decisions. In any case, if you need energy when you feel it is lacking, use this ritual and there should be a noticeable improvement. This new depth of energy does not need to be topped up like a battery. It makes a connection to a deeper source of energy that can last for many years and will only weaken if your circumstances change. If your circumstances do change (because you are required to put in more effort or make a life change), you may choose to repeat the ritual at a later date.

El is pronounced as ELL.
El Shaddai is pronounced as ELL-SHAD-EYE.
Qelileqaliah is pronounced as KELL-EE-LEK-AH-LEE-AH.
Michael is pronounced as MEEK-AH-ELL.
Orpaniel is pronounced as OAR-PAH-NEE-ELL.
Migael is pronounced as ME-GAH-ELL.
Mahash is pronounced as MAH-HAHSH.

ELL
ELL-SHAD-EYE
KELL-EE-LEK-AH-LEE-AH
MEEK-AH-ELL
OAR-PAH-NEE-ELL
ME-GAH-ELL
MAH-HAHSH

Protection from Negative Attachments

There are friends and family who can hurt you because of your history with them, and because of the emotional effects they have on you. Even well-meaning and loving people can become a form of negative attachment.

If you have experienced this, you probably need no further explanation. If not, then be aware that some relationships can create an attachment that makes you feel guilty, unworthy, or uneasy when you are around the other person. In such cases, you don't want to sever the bond, but to bring protection from the negativity it brings.

No single ritual will heal all the ills of a relationship because human connections are woven and transformed over many years. A relationship may need your continual attention, but this ritual will protect you from the negative feelings it creates.

The most common problem is when adults are treated like children by their parents. Another example is when a friend has made a judgment which, although supposedly forgotten, remains present in your interactions. Sometimes you won't know what the problem is, but you will know that a relationship brings bad feelings up for you. This ritual will protect you from the negativity, and enable you to maintain the relationship, perhaps even improving it to the point where there is no need for protection.

The rituals in this book only need to be performed once for any situation, but this may need to be repeated every few months if the underlying cause is unresolved and if you feel the negativity return.

El is pronounced as ELL.
El Shaddai is pronounced as ELL-SHAD-EYE.
Qelileqaliah is pronounced as KELL-EE-LEK-AH-LEE-AH.
Michael is pronounced as MEEK-AH-ELL.
Orpaniel is pronounced as OAR-PAH-NEE-ELL.
Povon is pronounced as PAW-VAWN.
Mahash is pronounced as MAH-HAHSH.

ELL
ELL-SHAD-EYE
KELL-EE-LEK-AH-LEE-AH
MEEK-AH-ELL
OAR-PAH-NEE-ELL
PAW-VAWN
MAH-HAHSH

Reconnect with Your Soul

It was mentioned in *The Ritual of Transformation* that there is no need to heal the soul, as it cannot be damaged, but we all know what it means to seek soul-healing. When you feel damaged or exhausted, with those feelings going deeper than your bones, right down to your soul, that is when you need to reconnect with your soul. You can, of course, use this ritual before things become drastic. If you feel yourself becoming drained, uncertain, or unsure of who you are or why you're here, rather than struggling on until you are about to reach breaking point, use this ritual.

In all the rituals, you need to contemplate the pain or discomfort you feel, and with this ritual, it is sometimes clear what feelings you want to overcome. At other times, however, it can be more abstract. You just feel out of sorts or unsure of yourself. In such cases, when you are contemplating the change you desire, notice how you feel, and consider whether or not this is a disconnection from your soul. You are not actually trying to form a judgment or answer, but in thinking about your soul and your connection to it, you become aware of the required feelings. When it comes to imagining the relief, you only need to imagine how empowered and peaceful you will feel when you have reconnected with your soul.

We are never truly disconnected from the soul, but often distant from it. Our awareness can become remote from the soul. This ritual is about letting the depths of the soul feed your mind, and nourish your being, so you regain a strong sense of who you are. The connection can be healing, peaceful and powerful, or in some cases it may only restore normality, but that could be all you need.

El is pronounced as ELL.
El Shaddai is pronounced as ELL-SHAD-EYE.
Iaheseiah is pronounced as EE-AH-EH-SEH-EE-AH.
Aniel is pronounced as AH-NEE-YELL.
Orpaniel is pronounced as OAR-PAH-NEE-ELL.
Zakeriel is pronounced as ZAH-KEH-REE-YELL.
Reho is pronounced as REH-HAW.

ELL
ELL-SHAD-EYE
EE-AH-EH-SEH-EE-AH
AH-NEE-YELL
OAR-PAH-NEE-ELL
ZAH-KEH-REE-YELL
REH-HAW

Find Peace When There is Disruption

When a changing situation has become difficult, but not completely overwhelming, you can think of it as a disruption. While often necessary, such disruption can be unpleasant, and you may need to connect with your inner serenity. This helps you get through without it all being too stressful.

For situations of complete overwhelm, there is a different ritual called *Find Peace When Overwhelmed*, as the experience of overwhelm is more intense and debilitating than that of disruption. With disruption, I am talking about times when you may be changing your job, moving house, or experiencing a life change that was in no way expected. If this disruption is bearable, you don't need the ritual, but if it's interfering with your level of peace, this ritual will bring relief when it is needed.

El is pronounced as ELL.
El Shaddai is pronounced as ELL-SHAD-EYE.
Iaheseiah is pronounced as EE-AH-EH-SEH-EE-AH.
Aniel is pronounced as AH-NEE-YELL.
Orpaniel is pronounced as OAR-PAH-NEE-ELL.
Agdelen is pronounced as AHG-DEH-LEN.
Reho is pronounced as REH-HAW.

ELL
ELL-SHAD-EYE
EE-AH-EH-SEH-EE-AH
AH-NEE-YELL
OAR-PAH-NEE-ELL
AHG-DEH-LEN
REH-HAW

Ease Self-Destructive Behavior

You'll have noticed that this ritual doesn't aim to eradicate self-destructive behavior, and there's a reason. When a behavior that harms you is eased, it can be integrated into your life as something useful. If, for example, you procrastinate, eradicating the very concept of procrastination might mean you would lose touch with the ability to be lazy from time to time. Being able to take time out is important.

If you have a behavior such as habitual over-eating, eradicating that completely would mean you might never enjoy a large and indulgent meal. The ritual works in a way that makes a behavior lessen until it is no longer destructive to you, and it does this by breaking the feeling of habit associated with the behavior. It also makes you more aware of the behavior, giving you a moment in which you can make a decision about whether to repeat the behavior or not. And in those moments, the ritual gives you the strength to make a decision that *lessens* the power the behavior has over you. This isn't about breaking addictions, but interrupting habits, to give you the choice to act in a more beneficial way.

You can focus on a behavior that you know is currently destructive, or you can aim the ritual more broadly, knowing you have undefined or unclear destructive behaviors, with the aim of finding relief by discerning and easing them.

El is pronounced as ELL.
El Shaddai is pronounced as ELL-SHAD-EYE.
Iaheseiah is pronounced as EE-AH-EH-SEH-EE-AH.
Aniel is pronounced as AH-NEE-YELL.
Orpaniel is pronounced as OAR-PAH-NEE-ELL.
Ravemaphi is pronounced as RAH-VEM-AH-FEE.
Reho is pronounced as REH-HAW.

ELL
ELL-SHAD-EYE
EE-AH-EH-SEH-EE-AH
AH-NEE-YELL
OAR-PAH-NEE-ELL
RAH-VEM-AH-FEE
REH-HAW

Turn Loneliness into Connection

Loneliness is experienced by people who are not alone, as well as those who suffer from social isolation. It is possible to feel lonely when in a relationship or when surrounded by friends, as well as when you are cut off from the world by circumstances. If you feel lonely, it can be because of the way you feel about yourself, the difficulty you have connecting with others, and a host of other emotional states. The beauty of this ritual is that you don't need to dissect your life to work out where the feeling comes from.

Perform this ritual, and whether the loneliness is caused by broken connections to people, or by circumstances that make you isolated from others, you will be given a chance to connect or reconnect with people that you like. You should notice a shift in your feelings toward people, and a willingness to seek out connections. The magick will help make you feel confident and willing to connect with people, while giving you opportunities to do so.

It is no secret that online interaction has taken the place of conversation, eye-contact and shared laughter, contributing to an increase in loneliness at all levels of modern society. You should make every effort to be with people in the real world. Being in the presence of another person, even if you don't know them well, is far more warming for the soul than typing up another online conversation.

The magick won't ban you from social media, but when you choose to be in the presence of people, the magick will make it easier to form the warm bonds that extinguish loneliness.

El is pronounced as ELL.
El Shaddai is pronounced as ELL-SHAD-EYE.
Iaheseiah is pronounced as EE-AH-EH-SEH-EE-AH.
Aniel is pronounced as AH-NEE-YELL.
Orpaniel is pronounced as OAR-PAH-NEE-ELL.
Ikahti is pronounced as EEK-AH-TEE.
Reho is pronounced as REH-HAW.

ELL
ELL-SHAD-EYE
EE-AH-EH-SEH-EE-AH
AH-NEE-YELL
OAR-PAH-NEE-ELL
EEK-AH-TEE
REH-HAW

Find Affinity with an Enemy

With this ritual, you are able to find common ground with somebody that you consider to be an enemy. You can use this common ground to remove the enmity and make peace. If that is what you seek from this ritual, there is nothing more to it than that, and you'll find it can be one of the best ways to make a simmering hatred or ongoing friction ease into something altogether more pleasant. If the person you consider to be an enemy shows signs of relenting, you do not need to try to be best friends, but you should respond to any peace offering with warmth. Remain cautious, but be warm, to encourage the enmity to fade. There are many rituals in magick for binding and harming enemies, but sometimes all you want is peace.

El is pronounced as ELL.
El Shaddai is pronounced as ELL-SHAD-EYE.
Iaheseiah is pronounced as EE-AH-EH-SEH-EE-AH.
Aniel is pronounced as AH-NEE-YELL.
Orpaniel is pronounced as OAR-PAH-NEE-ELL.
Areniel is pronounced as AH-REN-EE-YELL.
Reho is pronounced as REH-HAW.

ELL
ELL-SHAD-EYE
EE-AH-EH-SEH-EE-AH
AH-NEE-YELL
OAR-PAH-NEE-ELL
AH-REN-EE-YELL
REH-HAW

Discover Limiting Flaws

One of the most difficult things you can do is look within to see your flaws. It's like asking somebody close to you to tell you honestly how you could improve yourself, and then being devastated when they give you a long list of unexpected criticisms. It will take courage to use this ritual because when you do, you will become aware of your flaws.

There is compassion here, and the ritual does not make you feel guilty or ashamed of who you are but is directed only at revealing the flaws that limit your progress. That means that if you are trying to live in a certain way, or achieve particular things, and there are flaws in the way, you will be made aware of them.

Usually, this awareness occurs to you as a thought, feeling, or growing sensation, but sometimes you may experience a moment where you act in a certain way and for the first time you see things differently. It's almost like seeing yourself in the third person, and realizing that what you're doing is not in your best interest.

The ritual won't make you give up all your bad habits or uncover every weakness or quirk of personality, but will gently bring your awareness to the areas you need to look at if you want to achieve everything you can.

El is pronounced as ELL.
El Shaddai is pronounced as ELL-SHAD-EYE.
Iaheseiah is pronounced as EE-AH-EH-SEH-EE-AH.
Aniel is pronounced as AH-NEE-YELL.
Orpaniel is pronounced as OAR-PAH-NEE-ELL.
Mavet is pronounced as MAH-VET.
Reho is pronounced as REH-HAW.

ELL
ELL-SHAD-EYE
EE-AH-EH-SEH-EE-AH
AH-NEE-YELL
OAR-PAH-NEE-ELL
MAH-VET
REH-HAW

End a Period of Misfortune

You will have noticed that *The Ritual of Transformation* will often end a period of misfortune by itself, but if you need that result urgently or as a priority, it is worth using this ritual to bring a period of disturbance to an end.

The ritual works whether the misfortune has been brought about by the ill will of others, something within you, or because sometimes the bad events in life all pile up at once. When these situations dominate your life, they can build momentum and make it feel like bad luck will never end. Throughout our books, there are several rituals to end bad luck, but what I like about this one is that it calls on the Angels to bring you a feeling of relief even before the events are under control.

It may take some time to sort out the details of your reality so that the apparent misfortune is gone, but the relief should come quickly. This doesn't mean there's an illusion of wellbeing but that you connect to the feelings of the near-future when the period of misfortune will have ended. And then, the misfortune will ease away. You will never be protected from all misfortune, but this ritual also strengthens you so that when the next few mishaps occur, you don't assume you've fallen back into a rut of misfortune.

El is pronounced as ELL.
El Shaddai is pronounced as ELL-SHAD-EYE.
Iaheseiah is pronounced as EE-AH-EH-SEH-EE-AH.
Aniel is pronounced as AH-NEE-YELL.
Orpaniel is pronounced as OAR-PAH-NEE-ELL.
Ketiviah is pronounced as KEH-TEE-VEE-AH.
Reho is pronounced as REH-HAW.

ELL
ELL-SHAD-EYE
EE-AH-EH-SEH-EE-AH
AH-NEE-YELL
OAR-PAH-NEE-ELL
KEH-TEE-VEE-AH
REH-HAW

Strengthen Personal Confidence

When people talk about self-confidence, I think it generates an uneasy feeling as though you are building up your ego, or even worse, putting on a mask of confidence. I prefer to think of our personal confidence as the authentic pleasure of being who we are when we are not betrayed by doubts, fears, or judgments.

Those dark feelings that quash confidence come from within, from the comments and statements of others, and from a long history of trying to assess who we are. You can use this ritual to strengthen your personal confidence by removing the barriers that enable you to connect with your core being.

A lack of confidence can result in a shy personality or can make outwardly confident people feel conflicted. For many others, damaged personal confidence can lead to poor decisions, doubts and an inability to pursue your dreams. Strengthening your personal confidence is not about becoming boastful, but feeling the strength of the self that lies beneath your history and personality. For some people, using magick gives them an insight into this strength for the first time.

El is pronounced as ELL.
El Shaddai is pronounced as ELL-SHAD-EYE.
Sabkasbeiah is pronounced as SAB-KASS-BEH-EE-AH.
Amediel is pronounced as AM-EH-DEE-YELL.
Orpaniel is pronounced as OAR-PAH-NEE-ELL.
Parokeh is pronounced as PAH-RAW-KEH.
Eshal is pronounced as ESH-AHL.

ELL
ELL-SHAD-EYE
SAB-KASS-BEH-EE-AH
AM-EH-DEE-YELL
OAR-PAH-NEE-ELL
PAH-RAW-KEH
ESH-AHL

Strengthen Willpower Over Temptation

If you are suffering from an addiction, you will always need professional help and the support of friends and family. You need to change your environment as well. If you need to give up drinking, hanging out with your friends who drink is not going to work. Addiction is a complex subject with many causes. It requires professional intervention. For those who work with magick, the power of the Angels can bring greater willpower to your efforts, but it can never work without outside help. If you are struggling with a major addiction, you will need all the help you can get and allowing Angelic magick to support you may be wise.

The ritual will also work for people who are not addicts, but who succumb to temptation more than they want. I don't need to list the temptations that may be harming you because you know when pleasure has turned into over-indulgence. If you want the willpower to resist this temptation, use the ritual to feel the relief you would feel if you were able to overcome the habit of temptation.

El is pronounced as ELL.
El Shaddai is pronounced as ELL-SHAD-EYE.
Sabkasbeiah is pronounced as SAB-KASS-BEH-EE-AH.
Amediel is pronounced as AM-EH-DEE-YELL.
Orpaniel is pronounced as OAR-PAH-NEE-ELL.
Akielah is pronounced as AH-KEE-ELL-AH.
Eshal is pronounced as ESH-AHL.

ELL
ELL-SHAD-EYE
SAB-KASS-BEH-EE-AH
AM-EH-DEE-YELL
OAR-PAH-NEE-ELL
AH-KEE-ELL-AH
ESH-AHL

Improve Leadership Abilities

This ritual works for leaders who wish to improve their skills, and also for those developing these skills for the first time. To see the benefits, you will need to be in situations where you are able to exercise those skills. Leadership is about inspiration, communication, and trust, more than the ability to convince or control people. This ritual not only helps you develop those skills (as you study the subject of leadership) but enables you to project a confident sense of authority that generates admiration. This aspect of the ritual is important because many people find that when they act like a leader, it can create feelings of fear, resentment, and mistrust in those you want to lead. By conveying an aura that makes you seem admirable, people are much more likely to enjoy seeing and trusting you to be a leader.

El is pronounced as ELL.
El Shaddai is pronounced as ELL-SHAD-EYE.
Sabkasbeiah is pronounced as SAB-KASS-BEH-EE-AH.
Amediel is pronounced as AM-EH-DEE-YELL.
Orpaniel is pronounced as OAR-PAH-NEE-ELL.
Bavamadi is pronounced as BAH-VAH-MAH-DEE.
Eshal is pronounced as ESH-AHL.

ELL
ELL-SHAD-EYE
SAB-KASS-BEH-EE-AH
AM-EH-DEE-YELL
OAR-PAH-NEE-ELL
BAH-VAH-MAH-DEE
ESH-AHL

Endure Stasis in Peace

Magick is often about making things happen when you want them to happen, so why would you want to endure anything? The ritual was designed for those times when, no matter how powerful you might be, you have no choice but to wait. If you're waiting for the results of a cancer biopsy, or some other medical condition, or any news that could change your life, the wait can be almost unendurable. In situations like this, where you have to go through a period of waiting, allow this ritual to bring you peace so that it doesn't feel like endurance. It won't take away your concerns but will make you feel at peace with them, instead of cycling through worry, or obsessing constantly and wishing the time away. It won't change the outcome of the news, or whatever it is you are waiting for, but it will make the wait more bearable and less draining.

El is pronounced as ELL.
El Shaddai is pronounced as ELL-SHAD-EYE.
Sabkasbeiah is pronounced as SAB-KASS-BEH-EE-AH.
Amediel is pronounced as AM-EH-DEE-YELL.
Orpaniel is pronounced as OAR-PAH-NEE-ELL.
Amok is pronounced as AH-MAWK.
Eshal is pronounced as ESH-AHL.

ELL
ELL-SHAD-EYE
SAB-KASS-BEH-EE-AH
AM-EH-DEE-YELL
OAR-PAH-NEE-ELL
AH-MAWK
ESH-AHL

Increase the Momentum of Your Efforts

Impatience is the enemy of magick so much of the time, but it is to be expected that when you are working toward a goal, you may want to increase the speed at which your efforts manifest results. This isn't always the case. If you are wise, you will know that *some* work should develop slowly, so that you have time to understand and respond to all changes.

This ritual is for the times when you feel things are moving too slowly, and that given the effort you are putting into a project, things should be moving faster. This applies to any situation where you are putting in an active effort. You may be writing a novel, building a business, developing a relationship, or trying to publicize your product. If it feels like things are moving too slowly, let this ritual release the energy of your efforts to bring more momentum to your reality.

El is pronounced as ELL.
El Shaddai is pronounced as ELL-SHAD-EYE.
Sabkasbeiah is pronounced as SAB-KASS-BEH-EE-AH.
Amediel is pronounced as AM-EH-DEE-YELL.
Orpaniel is pronounced as OAR-PAH-NEE-ELL.
Paavar is pronounced as PAH-AH-VAHR.
Eshal is pronounced as ESH-AHL.

ELL
ELL-SHAD-EYE
SAB-KASS-BEH-EE-AH
AM-EH-DEE-YELL
OAR-PAH-NEE-ELL
PAH-AH-VAHR
ESH-AHL

Clear Dark Energies from a Location

Some people are sensitive to the energies of a location and will know when something bad is lingering there. Other people may not sense much but will know a place doesn't feel quite right. In any situation where a place doesn't feel right to you, especially if it's your home, use this ritual. Perform the ritual in the location that feels unpleasant.

The dark energies are not necessarily as frightening as you may think, so this won't be a scene like something from a horror movie, where the darkness fights back. The ritual has been designed so that the Angels only cleanse the space of energies that are by their nature dark. It will not banish all spirits, energies or presences; only those that bring harm or darkness. It is not a complete banishing, but a way of making a place that feels unusual or strange feel normal again.

If there are extremely dark energies, such as spirits sent by a curse, hauntings, or painful memories that have taken on a life of their own, the ritual will work against those as well. But in most cases, dark energies are usually just the aftermath of unpleasant situations that occurred in the location. Don't concern yourself with what the dark energy may be. Only focus on how it makes you feel, and the relief you will feel when it is gone.

El is pronounced as ELL.
El Shaddai is pronounced as ELL-SHAD-EYE.
Sabkasbeiah is pronounced as SAB-KASS-BEH-EE-AH.
Amediel is pronounced as AM-EH-DEE-YELL.
Orpaniel is pronounced as OAR-PAH-NEE-ELL.
Barok is pronounced as BAH-RAWK.
Eshal is pronounced as ESH-AHL.

ELL
ELL-SHAD-EYE
SAB-KASS-BEH-EE-AH
AM-EH-DEE-YELL
OAR-PAH-NEE-ELL
BAH-RAWK
ESH-AHL

Protect Against Energy Thieves

You may have noticed that some people drain your energy. Being around them leaves them filled with enthusiasm and vigor, while you feel drained. Sometimes this is intentional craft worked by a subtle occultist, but many energy thieves are ordinary people who have acquired this unpalatable skill without even knowing. Whether intentional or not, such people steal your energy, which empowers them at your expense. You will find energy thieves at work, in business, amongst friends, and even with some passing acquaintances.

You can use this ritual against a specific person if you know of somebody who drains you in this way. It will not make that person stop looking at you. It will not make them move out of your life unless their sole intention is to feed off your energy. In most cases, it will remove their power to take energy from you and will restore a balance so that you can be together without being drained.

If you feel that somebody is draining your energy, but you have no idea who that person may be, you can still use this ritual. Instead of directing it at a single person, use the ritual to shield yourself against all who would drain you of energy.

If you have relationships that are draining by their nature, such as an intense romance, or if you're looking after children, this ritual will not help. Those situations are exhausting because they are so demanding, and this ritual is only aimed at the supernatural energy theft that sometimes occurs.

El is pronounced as ELL.
El Shaddai is pronounced as ELL-SHAD-EYE.
Sabkasbeiah is pronounced as SAB-KASS-BEH-EE-AH.
Amediel is pronounced as AM-EH-DEE-YELL.
Orpaniel is pronounced as OAR-PAH-NEE-ELL.
Gilen is pronounced as GEE-LEN.
Eshal is pronounced as ESH-AHL.

ELL
ELL-SHAD-EYE
SAB-KASS-BEH-EE-AH
AM-EH-DEE-YELL
OAR-PAH-NEE-ELL
GEE-LEN
ESH-AHL

Attract Help When in Need

When you are in need, all you should have to do is ask for help, but there are times when it seems like nobody is available. Everybody makes an excuse, and during a difficult time you can feel isolated and abandoned even if you have extensive family and many friends. When this happens, it can be a coincidence, or it may be caused by some underlying energy between yourself and others. Whatever causes the situation you can reverse it with this ritual. Feel the need for help, but don't direct it at anybody specific. This leaves the magick more open to possibility, and if you allow help to come from anywhere, then some help will come.

This might sound like a power you would never use, but I have known many people who were struggling to meet all the demands made of them, and all they needed was a little help from family or friends. The ritual may even attract new people into your life who can assist.

The ritual is not designed to find people who might want to help you start a business, or work on a project. It is there for those times when life becomes overwhelming, and you need the help of others, even if only briefly, to get you through.

El is pronounced as ELL.
El Shaddai is pronounced as ELL-SHAD-EYE.
Sabkasbeiah is pronounced as SAB-KASS-BEH-EE-AH.
Amediel is pronounced as AM-EH-DEE-YELL.
Orpaniel is pronounced as OAR-PAH-NEE-ELL.
Arenoveh is pronounced as AH-REN-AWE-VEH.
Eshal is pronounced as ESH-AHL.

ELL
ELL-SHAD-EYE
SAB-KASS-BEH-EE-AH
AM-EH-DEE-YELL
OAR-PAH-NEE-ELL
AH-REN-AWE-VEH
ESH-AHL

Dismiss the Will of an Enemy

The ritual works most effectively when you know the name and intent of your enemy. You don't speak their name, of course, but you picture them and think of them during the ritual, and this targets the magick directly.

Use this ritual to dismiss their willpower, their anger and hatred, and their willingness to hurt you. There is a casual feeling about this, where you allow your power to swat your enemy aside. When you feel the relief from the ritual, it will have an immediate effect on your enemy, although the full effects, where the actions and responses of that person become obvious, may take longer.

You can also use this against a group of people that you consider to be enemies, even if you don't know their name. If you suspect one enemy is trying to undermine you, the ritual can be used even when you have no idea who that person is. In situations like this, you don't need to picture the specific person or think of their name or label the group in any way. You only contemplate the feeling that this enemy (whether a group or an individual,) generates in you, and that will direct the ritual.

El is pronounced as ELL.
El Shaddai is pronounced as ELL-SHAD-EYE.
Sabkasbeiah is pronounced as SAB-KASS-BEH-EE-AH.
Amediel is pronounced as AM-EH-DEE-YELL.
Orpaniel is pronounced as OAR-PAH-NEE-ELL.
Kapon is pronounced as KAP-AWN.
Eshal is pronounced as ESH-AHL.

ELL
ELL-SHAD-EYE
SAB-KASS-BEH-EE-AH
AM-EH-DEE-YELL
OAR-PAH-NEE-ELL
KAP-AWN
ESH-AHL

Inspire Strangers to Admire You

If you want to be admired in life, generally, so that strangers find you fascinating and see you as approachable, you can use this ritual to achieve that effect. Be warned, however, that you may attract more attention than you want. It doesn't guarantee that people will be clamoring for your attention, because a lot of that depends upon how you present yourself, but it will make people look at you and be inspired to know you because they feel a sense of admiration, even if they don't understand why.

A more practical use, perhaps, is when you are promoting yourself to the world at large and wish to be admired. In some respects, this is similar to the ritual to *Attract a Following*, but here it is driven by people admiring your personality rather than your work. Again, this can be a double-edged sword, because it is your personality they will attach to. For some people this is ideal, but in other cases, you may want your character to remain in the background while people focus on your work. Choose your magick carefully.

El is pronounced as ELL.
El Shaddai is pronounced as ELL-SHAD-EYE.
Sabkasbeiah is pronounced as SAB-KASS-BEH-EE-AH.
Amediel is pronounced as AM-EH-DEE-YELL.
Orpaniel is pronounced as OAR-PAH-NEE-ELL.
Apatiel is pronounced as AH-PAH-TEE-YELL.
Eshal is pronounced as ESH-AHL.

ELL
ELL-SHAD-EYE
SAB-KASS-BEH-EE-AH
AM-EH-DEE-YELL
OAR-PAH-NEE-ELL
AH-PAH-TEE-YELL
ESH-AHL

Make the Unwanted Stay Away

This is not a ritual designed to make somebody leave a shared house or workplace, but makes an unwanted person lose interest in you. If there's an unwanted friend that keeps visiting or somebody that keeps asking you out, you can use this ritual to make them stay away from you. It can be a good way to ease somebody away from your life without a confrontation.

In more extreme cases, where there is somebody hateful, violent or dangerous, the ritual can also help to provide protection by making the person stay away from you, but ensure you also take mundane actions as well, such as calling the police.

Another use for the ritual is in situations where you are being pestered or harassed online, either by somebody who is deliberately trying to annoy you or by somebody who has become overly fascinated with you. In most cases, you can handle this without magick, but if somebody is uncomfortably persistent, you can make them less likely to bother you with this ritual.

El is pronounced as ELL.
El Shaddai is pronounced as ELL-SHAD-EYE.
Sabkasbeiah is pronounced as SAB-KASS-BEH-EE-AH.
Amediel is pronounced as AM-EH-DEE-YELL.
Orpaniel is pronounced as OAR-PAH-NEE-ELL.
Tiamiel is pronounced as TEE-AH-ME-YELL.
Eshal is pronounced as ESH-AHL.

ELL
ELL-SHAD-EYE
SAB-KASS-BEH-EE-AH
AM-EH-DEE-YELL
OAR-PAH-NEE-ELL
TEE-AH-ME-YELL
ESH-AHL

Speaking the Words of Power

Mystical Words of Power is absolutely Pronunciation Proof. When you scan the letters visually, that does more than half the work, so you don't need to get the pronunciation perfectly correct. If you can make an approximate sound, that helps, which is why the vocalization is included. But you don't need to get everything perfectly right.

The pronunciations are not always objectively correct, but we have found pronunciations that work easily for western speakers, and that produce the desired effect. That is what you find here. If you have any problems, there's a video on The Gallery of Magick website (**www.galleryofmagick.com**) that lets you hear how this works. You can find it on the *Pronunciation and Spelling FAQ* page. Most of the time, you won't need it because the pronunciation is not difficult.

The key is to speak the words in capitals as though they are English. So, you may see a word such as this:

AM-EH-DEE-YELL

This is one word, made up of several sounds. You read the sounds as though they are English. That would be as follows:

AM is just the word **am.**

EH is the **e** sound in **net**, as described below

DEE is like the word **deer** without the **r.**

YELL is the word **yell.**

Run these together, and you get AM-EH-DEE-YELL. As you can see, it is quite easy to work out how to say the sounds, by finding an English equivalent.

Sometimes you need to take a familiar English sound and add something to it, as with the sound **SAB**, for example. You know that **AB** sounds like **cab** without the **c**, so you put **s** in front of the **ab** sound to get **SAB**.

If you see **RAWG**, you know this is the word **raw** with the **g** sound added at the end. It's very easy and takes just a few minutes to learn the words for each ritual.

Throughout this book you will see El Shaddai, pronounced as ELL-SHAD-EYE. I will use this as a final example. ELL is **bell** without the **b**. SHAD is **shadow** without the **ow** sound. EYE is the English word **eye**. It takes some effort to understand the sounds, but not much, and given the power within these rituals it is worth taking a few minutes to get used to the required words.

To make it easier, it's worth looking at some of the more commonly used sounds in this book. If these are even close to being correct, you'll be doing a great job.

UH

UH is **up** without the **p**. So, if you see the sound **KUH**, you know that it sounds like **cup** without the **p**.

AH

The **AH** sound is like the **ah** you get in **ma** and **pa**. When you say **ma** without the **m**, you've got the right sound.

EH

EH is like the middle part of the word **net**. Say **net** without the **n** or the **t**, and you've got **EH**.

AW or AWE

AW is **raw** without the **r**. If you see **CAW**, you know it sounds like the word **awe** with **c** at the beginning.

AY

AY is like **pay** without the **p**. If you see **NAY**, it's like **pay** with **n** instead of **p**.

G

G sounds like the **g** in **give**, rather than the **g** in **gem**. So **GAH** sounds like the first part of **garlic**, before you get to **rlic**.

TZ

TZ is like the end of the word **cats**. If you think of it as **catz**, that's even better.

CH

Hebrew often uses the **ch** sound that you hear in the Scottish word **loch** or the German **achtung**. Our video reveals the sound you want to achieve. Alternatively, you can simply make a **K** sound when you see **CH**.

To illustrate this, you will have seen the sound **CHEK**. This is not like the word **check**. Instead, it is the **CH** sound described above, followed by **EK**. If you can't make the guttural **ch** sound, then replace it with a **k**. So **CHEK** becomes **KEK**.

This may seem complicated, but remember that for the most part, you are reading English sounds, and if you remain relaxed about it, you will have access to powerful magick.

The only real challenge is **CH,** and even that doesn't have to be perfect. You can try for the correct sounding **CH**, or sound it as **K** instead. It's fine to do that, and even some highly experienced occultists used **K** instead of the **CH** sound.

The book is Pronunciation Proof, and it is perfectly safe to practice the words before you actually come to perform a ritual. I would recommend that you take the time to do this so you can feel relaxed about the ritual itself.

If you've already worked with *Words of Power* or *The Greater Words of Power*, you'll see that some words appear in both books, but are pronounced differently here. This is intentional, and you don't need to change how you work with the other books.

The Origin of The Words

While some of these Divine words and Angelic names are known to occultists, some are less frequently encountered. You may want to know what it all means and where it comes from.

It is difficult to explain the origin of the words without giving a complete history of magick and all associated theory. What I can say is that there are many magickal systems, and often they have a shared origin. There are many personal grimoires, for example, that describe the same Angels found in mystical Jewish texts. There are also thousands of inconsistencies and contradictions.

Although we have been able to employ a technique called speculative evocation, to contact spirits such as Angels, and question them regarding their powers, their names and so on, that is a highly demanding form of magick, and it works best when you have almost perfected your research. There are seventeen members of The Gallery of Magick, and we have all done a lot of reading and research. We've also purchased private collections of occult materials, and as has been noted by many authors, the seemingly minor additions that are bundled in with these collections are often a source of original knowledge. If this 'secret' knowledge is later found elsewhere, we can assume it has a common origin. Such a discovery doesn't guarantee that it works, but implies it is worthy of investigation.

With all that said, I can say that the majority of the techniques in this book arise from traditions of Kabbalah (which is in a constant state of development, rather than stasis) while referencing ancient texts such as *Brit Menucha* and *Shorshei ha-Shemot*. We also suspected that there was great potential in the book *Sefer ha-Razim*, even though it was dismissed by many academics. One problem with that book is that the vowel markings were missing from the Angelic names, and it was only when two further documents came into our possession that we were able to decode the purpose and true names of those Angels.

As you can see, there is no simple history when it comes to magick. And if the idea of private grimoires seems fanciful, you should take a look at the popular academic authors who have referenced many such grimoires, and are even now publishing translations of them. Privately held documents are one of the most important ways that a magickal group can develop its methods, but only if you are able to discern what is gold and what is mere glitter for fools.

The method for ordering the names in the sigils, as discussed earlier in the book, was arrived at by obtaining a manuscript created by somebody outside of our group, and it remains unclear whether that author invented the method or assembled it based on the encoded work of others (as I suspect.)

In the end, though, there is no substitute for practical magick, and the sigils found in these books were arrived at not through academic work or by deciphering codes, but by working with the magick, by evoking directly, and by seeing what worked, and what did not. Sometimes, the smallest change could transform an ordinary sigil into something special.

As you can imagine, developing this technique is not something that has happened overnight. It is possible, once you know the method, to put something together rapidly, but the sigils with the greatest power have taken many years to develop. And none of this is of any concern if you are able to get the magick to work. I have included this brief chapter to show that the deeper you dig, the deeper the mystery becomes, and as I have said so many times, ten minutes of magickal experience will probably teach you more than several months of research.

That doesn't mean we know the only way of creating sigils like this, and there may be others who have access to similar materials and secrets. But I think it's important to know that this is work that has taken decades to refine. It is something in which I have played my part, but I did not achieve this alone. I am grateful to all those who helped make this system so beautiful.

The Future of Magick

When I was growing up and heard the word *mystical* for the first time, I thought it meant the same as *mystery*. I don't want this book to be a mystery to you, and I hope that if you read it thoroughly and perform the rituals, you will have experiences that are interesting, useful and sometimes mystical. There is personal mystery in the process, and finding out what that means is different for everybody, but the magick in this book might help you make discoveries that give you mastery over your place in the universe.

A long time has passed, and I have spent most of my life involved with occultism. Magick is doing well, and it feels like more people than ever are finding ways to get magick working. Yes, there's some quackery, but that's always the case.

If you were drawn to this book, I hope you are able to get more out of it than you ever hoped. If not, I trust that you will wait until the time is right, because then you may find it is perfect for you. The magick shared in this book, especially the magick in Part One, is something very precious and dear to my heart.

Some readers may be upset because there isn't a sigil *To Have a Mystical Experience*, but I know that if you've tried the magick, you will understand why such an over-simplification would be fruitless. By performing the rituals and exploring the spiritual aspect of magick, the mystical can be found in ordinary moments, in visions, and in ways that can never be described in words. With patience, there is all the magick you need to obtain such experiences within the pages of this book.

I continue to believe that sharing occult knowledge is important, even in a time of widespread deception and fakery. I will enjoy these final few months of writing, putting into words all that I am permitted to share. Thank you for taking the time to explore this magick.

Damon Brand

www.galleryofmagick.com

Exploring Magick

If you have questions, our website is an excellent source of background material and practical posts that help you to get magick working. We could have published two or three books on magickal practice, but instead, it's all there for free.

You can also find extensive FAQs for every book. I urge you to make good use of the site when you encounter problems, and also when you wish to expand your understanding of magick.

I hope you use and enjoy the sigils in this book, but please note that they are not meant to be worn as amulets, worn on the body, turned into tattoos, put up on walls, or hidden in wallets. Their power comes not from being worn as jewelry or decoration, but by being used as described. These sigils are not in the public domain, so they should not be used for resale of any kind. To make personal copies, you can photocopy, photograph, or take screenshots and print them out, but I recommend using them on a device, computer screen or in the paperback.

If you have an interest in developing your magick further, there are many texts by The Gallery of Magick authors that can assist you.

Magickal Protection contains rituals that can be directed at specific problems, as well as a daily practice called The Sword Banishing, which is one of our most popular and effective rituals.

The Master Works of Chaos Magick is an overview of self-directed and creative magick, which also includes a section covering the Olympic Spirits.

The 72 Sigils of Power covers Contemplation Magic (for insight and wisdom) and Results Magic (for changing the world around you) which is by the author of *The Angels of Love*, to heal relationships and attract a soulmate.

Words of Power and *The Greater Words of Power* present a method similar to the one in this book, to bring about change in yourself and others, as well as attracting changed circumstances.

For those seeking more money, *Magickal Cashbook* uses a ritual to attract small bursts of money out of the blue, and works best not when you are desperate, but when you can approach the magick with a sense of enjoyment and pleasure. *Magickal Riches* is more comprehensive, with rituals for everything from gambling to sales. There is a master ritual to oversee magickal income. For the more ambitious, *Wealth Magick* contains a complex set of rituals for earning money by building a career. For those still trying to find their feet, there is *The Magickal Job Seeker*.

The 72 Angels of Magick explores hundreds of powers, and *The Angels of Alchemy* works with Angels for personal transformation, which can be the key to unlocking magick.

Archangels of Magick is the most complete book of magick we have published, covering sigils, divination, invocation, and evocation.

Our most successful book is *Sigils of Power and Transformation* by Adam Blackthorne, which has brought great results to many people.

www.galleryofmagick.com

Made in United States
Orlando, FL
28 December 2022